Clinton

Ireland: the Stories of Her History

Gregory tells Me
of Your Great Kindness!

Ireland: the Stories of Her History

Dennis P. Sommers

Foreword by Dr. Seamus Metress

iUniverse, Inc.
New York Lincoln Shanghai

Ireland: the Stories of Her History

Copyright © 2006 by Dennis P. Sommers

All rights reserved. No part of this book may be used or reproduced by any means, graphic, electronic, or mechanical, including photocopying, recording, taping or by any information storage retrieval system without the written permission of the publisher except in the case of brief quotations embodied in critical articles and reviews.

iUniverse books may be ordered through booksellers or by contacting:

iUniverse
2021 Pine Lake Road, Suite 100
Lincoln, NE 68512
www.iuniverse.com
1-800-Authors (1-800-288-4677)

ISBN-13: 978-0-595-38985-8 (pbk)
ISBN-13: 978-0-595-83368-9 (ebk)
ISBN-10: 0-595-38985-6 (pbk)
ISBN-10: 0-595-83368-3 (ebk)

Printed in the United States of America

This publication is dedicated to

My Family and Friends

With deepest heartfelt appreciation!

On Pembroke Road look out for my ghost,
Disheveled with shoes untied,
Playing through the railings with little children
Whose children have long since died.

Patrick Kavanagh from
"If Ever You Go to Dublin Town"

Contents

Acknowledgements

There are so many wonderful individuals who have touched my life in an extremely positive way that it would be impossible to name them all here. There are a few however who have contributed greatly to the production of this work and I would like to acknowledge them and thank them for their guidance, encouragement and expertise. First there is of course Dr. Seamus Metress who wrote the Foreword for this book and has been a Professor of Physical, Cultural, and Medical Anthopology at the University of Toledo for nearly four decades. Dr. Metress was one of my very first mentors from over thirty-five years ago and his profound influence, and my heart felt appreciation, could never be adequately expressed. He and his lovely wife Dr. Eileen Metress have been an incredible source of inspiration to thousands of developing minds, are highly competent scholars, and are both admirably dedicated to their students. I am extremely honored to have met them and call them my friends.

Other scholars who have been exceptionally supportive and influential include Professor Etienne Rynne of the University College Galway, a most knowledgeable authority regarding the archaeology of Celtic Ireland. He has mesmerized the students of the International Summer School at Trinity College Dublin as well with his profound explanations and personally guided tours through the National Museum of Ireland. I could never thank him enough. Also, I would like to express my deepest gratitude to two fellow members of the United Arts Club of Dublin, Ulick O'Connor and Kieran Devaney. Kieran Devaney is the editor of the six o'clock news in Dublin on TV3, and is a walking encyclopedia of knowledge and information, and has provided an insight and understanding of a quality few ever realize. Ulick O'Connor is without a doubt one of the most exceptional scholars, athlete, lecturer, author, and researcher the world has ever known. His accomplishments would fill this book and I thank him and Kieran dearly for the hours of exceptional conversation.

Foreword

✦

Telling a Story for the Ages

Dennis Sommers has written an interesting cultural history of Ireland in a very relaxed style. It is a brief yet instructive journey through the sweep of Irish history. Dr. Sommers presents us with a story that is glorious and tragic, yet inspiring and hopeful. It is a work that will interest the general reader as well as the serious student of Irish history. Sommers writes with conviction and enthusiasm rather than ponderous pomposity. He appears to be interested in communication and education rather than self promotion and academic image.

In ten pedagogically sound chapters he describes and analyzes the history of the Emerald Isle. He begins with a well organized foray into Irish prehistory, which is followed by discussing why Ireland is called the isle of Saints and Scholars. His survey of some of the major saints and the monastic roots of Irish Catholicism is interesting. Sommers' work on early Irish history shows why Ireland maintained cultural cohesion in the absence of political unity.

The book moves on to consider the culturally unsuccessful Norman and Viking invasions that were absorbed by Irish culture. Medieval Ireland, with the unsuccessful attempt at cultural apartheid, periodic risings and crown reactions, culminating in the Flight of the Earls, is a most informative discussion.

The plantation of Ulster by James I that established the early roots of sectarian division that plagues Ireland even today leads into the rising of 1641. He chronicles the rising of 1641 which left its indelible mark in Irish psychohistory, as Cromwell pursued a savage, genocidal campaign against the Irish people. But the rising did produce hints of Irish republicanism in the person of Owen Roe O'Neill whose premature death under mysterious circumstances doomed the Irish struggle and may have mightily altered the course of Irish history. Sommers also exposes the loyalist myth of a bloodbath in 1641. The tragedy of 1641 is followed by the battle of two foreign monarchs over the English throne on Irish soil. The Williamite war magnified the mythology of the sectarian divide that lingers heavily today during the marching season. The broken treaty that followed hostilities and eventually the Penal Laws laid the basis for the continued cultural genocide in Ireland. Sommers places all of these important events in vivid context.

The beginning of Irish republicanism among the United Irishmen led by Wolfe Tone, Henry Joy McCracken, Henry Munro and others, as well as their ill fated rising of 1798 is well done. The movement and memories of this rising still impact politics in Ireland today, with the rise of reactionary anti-catholic Orange Order during the era, which eventually emerged as a powerful force in a partitioned Ireland in the twentieth century. From 1798 and its idealism Sommers takes us through the O'Connell years, where he is kind to the boisterous landowner who didn't have the courage or the will to really free the Irish people. Yet he has been idolized by many as the founder of constitutional nationalism rather than a closet monarchist.

Dr. Sommers moves on to the tragedy of the Great Starvation with its hints of opportunistic genocide and horrendous memories of the starvation and emigration that affected Ireland, England and America for 150 years. The story takes us through the Young Irelanders and the Fenians who failed militarily but succeeded ideologically in the hearts of many. Parnell, Davitt and the Land League continue the Irish struggle for freedom from landlords as well as British rule late in the nineteenth century.

In the last three chapters Dr. Sommers guides us through the resurrection of Irishness and the role of the Gaelic League and the GAA. The founding of Sinn Fein and the heroic rising of Easter 1916, where the rebels snatched victory from defeat by a combination of English barbarism and rebel bravery, is well done. The failed rebellion of 1916 reawakened the Irish thirst for nationhood as evidenced by the Sinn Fein victory in the 1918 election. He moves through the brilliant war of Independence as well as the tragedy of the treaty and the Irish Civil war among republicans. This civil war taints Irish politics even today. It was a series of events that truly aborted the twentieth century's first true revolution.

The concluding discussion on Modern Ireland in relation to the partitioned part of Ireland's ancient territory is difficult to cover in a survey work such as this.

It is a story of how a minority "settler" population within a 30-mile radius of Belfast was allowed to determine the political fate of the majority of the island people through partition. The settler population within the artificial statelet then decided to systematically disenfranchise the Irish nationalist population of basic human rights. The partition of Ireland is a monument to the perversion of democratic principles by a modern western democracy.

Sommers is a thorough, sensitive scholar with the ability to interpret complex material for the general reader. He is an intelligent well organized, mature thinker. His work also testifies to his in depth knowledge with respect to the basics of Irish cultural history. From a readers point of view Sommers' work is a joy and an inspiration to read. The kind of work that makes the reader want to investigate further the topics and issues he presents.

—Dr. Seamus P. Metress

Introduction

History is studied for several different reasons, just as I'm certain all of you are reading this for your own particular reason. We can learn a great deal regarding human behavior, as well as social, political, religious, scholastic, and economic patterns and cycles that most arguably repeat themselves, at least in part. Ireland has a most ancient, unique, complex, and mystical history, which today has a good many of the world's scholars looking at Irish history. The profound influence of this small island on civilization and today's world is only now beginning to be understood. Many of the earliest inhabitants, dating to at least 8000 B.C.E. (B.C.) apparently had an extensive knowledge of mathematics, natural phenomena, astronomy and the movement of celestial bodies.

The Celtic peoples, including the Milesians and the Gaels, here discussed somewhat in Chapter One, were the most dominant culture north of the Alps from the beginning of European history until the first century B.C.E. and were masters of poetry, art, healing, spirituality, military efficiency, and learning. In Ireland they remained dominant for another thousand years and contributed to Ireland's great scholarship, mythology, folklore, religion, and lifestyle that were first recorded and perpetuated by the Christian monks through the early monasteries and their extremely dedicated scholastic endeavors.

Irish monasteries recorded and retained this knowledge, history and, in fact Christianity itself, when virtually the rest of Europe had lost the same to "barbarians" and pagan tribes. Monasteries such as those at Clonmacnois, Glendalough, Inishmore, and Armagh became huge centers of scholarship and spirituality, with thousands studying and teaching at each of them. The traveling monks then reintroduced these principles throughout Europe, and elsewhere, establishing monastic communities as the centers of learning, healing, scholarship, public service, and spirituality. The monasteries were the dominant societal forces throughout the Middle Ages in several regions, establishing many institutions that are still with us today. The early monasteries were virtually the first "cities" in Ireland and contributed greatly to the country's development.

The ancient Irish Celts were probably best known for their sophisticated command of the spoken word, which formed the basis for the extraordinary literary tradition to follow. This unique ability was probably what most fascinated the early Christian monks, who copied and preserved the stories and folklore. These traditions survived nowhere more specifically than in Ireland. This oral tradition was brought forth by the druids, bards, and poets (filid); and led latterly to literature and scholarship, which had by the seventh century stimulated pockets of intellectual activity in Europe that dominated the "Dark Ages", and greatly influenced all of medieval culture. It has indeed influenced literary pursuits to the present day.

A great many of the world's most accomplished writers have come from Ireland, and most readily acknowledge their Celtic and Irish traditional influences. The novel *Ulysses* by James Joyce has often been discussed as the greatest novel ever written, and one can easily see the intricate love of language, satire, stream of consciousness, and complex saga that Joyce employed; and, immediately attributed to his Irish/Gaelic influences. He was born in Dublin, as was Jonathan Swift, who two hundred years earlier displayed the same qualities in *Gulliver's Travels*. His biting satires of the inhuman English policies towards the Irish people spoke of the Celtic call for honor and equality, which have continued to echo through the ages ever since.

William Butler Yeats' masterful use of language has earned him the reputation among many scholars as being one of the top two writers ever in the English language. The W. B. Yeats International Summer School, drawing faculty, authors, and lecturers from the world's most renowned academic institutions, is considered by many to be the finest literary gathering in the western world. Yeats also founded the Abbey Theatre, along with fellow authors Lady Augusta Gregory, Dr. Douglas Hyde and John Millington Synge. W. B. Yeats won the Nobel Prize for Literature in 1923. The Nobel Prize for Literature was awarded in 1925 to another Irishman, George Bernard Shaw, also born in Dublin; and, in 1969 to yet another Dubliner, Samuel Beckett.

Trinity College, Dublin has long been considered one of the foremost literary schools in the world, training the likes of Samuel Beckett, Jonathan Swift, Thomas Moore, Edmund Burke (whose political philosophies formed the foundation of much of the American governmental system), George Berkeley, Thomas Davis, Oscar Wilde, Oliver Goldsmith, and countless others of eminent stature, as well as perhaps some of more infamous regard, such as Bram Stoker, the author of "Dracula", whose mother told him tales of the cholera epidemics in County Sligo, and the people who were thought to be dead only to later stir in their coffins. Dracula was originally titled "The Undead". In 1995, Seamus Heaney gave this small island the distinction of having as many Nobel Prize recipients in literature as any country in history.

In addition to the Celtic, monastic and literary influences, we will look at a variety of social, economic, and political factors shaping Ireland as well, including Britain's role in Irish politics and culture. We will discuss the struggle for Irish independence, look at modern Ireland, and examine some of the more recent events influencing people in both The Republic of Ireland and Northern Ireland as they attempt to build a future and implement the power-sharing provisions of the 1998 Belfast Agreement.

How did Ireland come to be called Ireland?

If you read the earliest accounts of the history of these westernmost European islands, it can become quite confusing. The island of Ireland is referred to by several different terms. The earliest writings—those basically prior to the Seventh Century—generally use the term Scotia for the island we now call Ireland, and Scot when referring to the Irish People. These terms of course later came to be applied to current Scotland, which at that time was called Alba or Pictland. The Greeks however, called this same island Keltal (island of the Keltoi, or Celts). Hibernia (or Ivernia) was the Latin name used by the Romans and prevalent in the writings of Julius Caesar and Roman historians prior to the fall of the Roman Empire.

The name Scotia was derived from the name Scota. Scota was the mythical queen/mother of the Milesian people, who invaded the island around 1000 B.C.E. (B.C.). Approximately 300 C.E. (A.D.), during the time of Constantine, his poet, Egesippus, termed Ireland Scotia, and this term was used by continental writers more than any other name for several hundred years. At the end of the Seventh Century the Irishman Adamnan, Abbot of Iona Monastery, referred to his home country as Scotia. As late as the eleventh century the famous Marianus Scotus (Marian the Scot) referred to the Irishmen as Scots. The Germanic author, Hermann, writing also in the eleventh century referred to them likewise as Scots.

Even in the Thirteenth Century, Caesar of Heisterbach, suggests people go to Scotia to visit St. Patrick's Purgatory, at that time, as it is yet today, a world-famous pilgrimage. St. Patrick's Purgatory is a cave in Loch Derg, County Donegal, where penitents have enclosed themselves for days or weeks in order to have visions of Heaven, Hell and Purgatory as St. Patrick had done. Today they are usually three-day or one-week pilgrimages.

The modern name for Ireland most likely first originated with the Norsemen, or Vikings, at the end of the Seventh Century. They referred to the island by the name of Ir or Ire, after one of their godly princes, and those on the continent slowly began referring to the island as Ireland. For several more centuries, however, the Irish scholars on the continent were called Scotus.

Adam De Breme, in the Eleventh Century, first promoted and popularized the term Ireland. The Term Scotland was then transferred to Alba because of the heavy colonization there by the Scots from the island, which began in the third century with the sons of Conaire the Great, King of Munster, and whom is often referred to as the High King of Ireland at that time (in reality there was no High King of Ireland during this period. That title wasn't claimed until hundreds of years afterward). They first settled the islands and coast of Argyle, as well as the northeast coast of County Antrim in Ireland, from where they initiated their crossings.

The Scotic (Irish) people eventually established dominance in what is now currently Scotland, as more and more came from Ireland to the aid of these first settlers helping to defend them against the aggressive attacks of the Picts, a northern European people thought to be a link between neolithic and Celtic peoples. The chieftain Fergus brought an army from what is now County Kerry in the Fifth Century. The Picts were continuously driven north and northeast, until 850, when they were completely overthrown by the King of Argyle, Cinead (Kenneth) MacAlpin, who became the first Gaelic King of Scotland.

Now that the Scots gained dominance over the land, it began to be called Scotia, at first Scotia Minor (Ireland was Scotia Major), but eventually the term Scotia became associated with only Alba. In the eleventh century many of the Angle, or early English people were pushed north in an attempt to flee the Norman Invasion. They settled southeastern Scotland, came into favor with the court at Edinburgh, and the old Irish, or Gaelic (latterly Gallic), Chieftains, were pushed to the highlands. The last Irish Royal lineage came to an end in 1287, when Alexander the Third died without an heir. This initiated the Wars of Succession between the lowland Old-English families and the Gaelic chieftains of the Highlands—Robert the Bruce, the Earl of Carrick, William Wallis, and all that.

But, since the late Middle Ages, the island first known as Scotia has been called Ireland by most of the world. Other names associated with the island include Eire, which is the Irish Gaelic word for Ireland and the official name as defined by the Irish Constitution of 1937. Erinn is the Old-English name for Ireland, with Erin being the modern poetic derivative.

Ancient Ireland

The history of Ireland indeed goes back to quite ancient times, and you can feel this often as you walk throughout the countryside. There are the ruins of many overlapping cultures, civilizations, and histories. The origins and nomenclature of the very oldest of these have probably been forever lost, but the spiritual presence of these long ago inhabitants can still in fact be realized in Ireland today. If you allow yourself the freedom, you can often sense that you are walking among long-dead mystics, kings, poets, druids, saints, artisans, warriors and farmers.

The first people came to Ireland approximately 10,000 years ago. Before that time Ireland's climate had been too arctic in nature to support human life. Between 11,000 and 12,000 B.C.E., the retreating ice sheet left Ireland a scoured out island of little more than rock and bog. Around 10,000 B.C.E., wild horses and giant deer (larger than modern-day elk) crossed what was then a land bridge between Ireland and modern Scotland. They multiplied basically unchecked until the first hunters arrived in approximately 6800 B.C.E.

By this time water from the melting arctic ice had risen to cover the land bridge, but the level was over seventy feet less than it is today and the crossing from Scotland to Ireland was only a mile or so wide and was easily negotiated in small dugout canoes. The climate was continuously moderating and by now there were tall forests covering much of the island. There was still however dry land between Britain and Scandinavia, and it is speculated that these first Mesolithic peoples may have come from that region.

The first Mesolithic Irishmen were small dark primitive hunters and gatherers who ate fish, birds, roots, berries, herbs and whatever they could find and/or kill. They used stone and flint tools. They roamed Ireland virtually unmolested for over 3000 years before the first Neolithic ("New Stone Age") peoples arrived—around 3900 B.C.E., probably from Gaul (modern France), or perhaps from the region of Cornwall. They cut clearings in the forests, domesticated the wild animals, built permanent structures, and began tilling the soil.

A stone circle dating from the Neolithic Period. These have been considered sacred throughout time, the Celtic druids conducted ceremonies here, and to this day these are not disturbed by farmers or landowners, believing only harm can come to those tampering with these ancient sites.

A representative Dolman of the Neolithic peoples found on the mountain of Knocknashee (the land of the fairies) in County Sligo.

Creevykeel Court Tomb, one of the best preserved court tombs in the world, dates from the fourth millennium B.C. Only rituals of very significant importance were conducted here. The site was excavated by Harvard University in 1935. Three tombs with cremated human remains were found at the western end, along with polished axe heads and Neolithic pottery. Creevykeel is located on the N-15 between Sligo and Bundoran.

By this time the climate was quite mild and agreeable, similar to what it is like today. Except for approximately fifty miles of beach located on the east coast, Ireland is virtually rimmed by mountains. Ireland's climate is primarily the result of the north Atlantic drift current and the Gulf Stream current (the same current that goes up the east coast of Florida and America, and then travels across the northern Atlantic Ocean). When these two meet, the cold and warm air vaporizes and produces a pure distilled mist or moisture over the island. This moisture gets trapped within the saucer-like interior formed by the mountains, and produces some of the most lush pastures and green vegetation to be found anywhere on earth. Hence, Ireland's famous forty shades of green.

Some of the earliest archaeological evidence of these first permanent structures may be found in the northwest of Ireland, at Carrowmore and Creevykeel in County Sligo, and at Ballynagilly in County Tyrone; and, in the Boyne River valley of County Meath. The first of these permanent settlements date to between 3700 and 4000 B.C.E. These early inhabitants used both rock and wood in construction (mostly oak, and from these earliest times there is evidence that oak trees were spiritually revered). These people were most famous however for the large stone monuments they constructed, called Dolmans, where they buried their dead and worshipped their gods. Some of the earliest of these are found in County Sligo, and on the high cliffs and in the fields overlooking Donegal Bay. These people also built large burial mounds, many of which can still be found all over Ireland. Some of the earliest and most elaborate (or at least well-preserved) of these are to be found in the Boyne River Valley in County Meath, namely at Nowth, Dowth, and Newgrange.

Newgrange, the most famous of these, is what is known as a "passage grave", with the cremated remains of its inhabitants being entombed at the ends of long tunnels, within a human-constructed mound consisting of thousands of tons of rock and earth. The tunnel at Newgrange is over sixty feet long and leads into a central area of three tombs shaped like a cross. At the entrances of these tunnels there are huge curbstones decorated with elaborate geometric designs, as are the rocks lining the insides of the passageways. The rocks lining the walls and ceilings of the tombs are even more ornamental with amazingly intricate patterns of circles, double-spirals, zigzags, herringbones, triangles and diamonds. It is believed that these designs held an astronomical importance, as all are aligned with the movements of the sun and stars, and on one day each year, that of the Winter Solstice, the sun's light enters the long passageway and reaches the internal tombs of Newgrange for precisely one minute. These early people most assuredly had an intricate understanding of nature, mathematics, and the movement of celestial bodies, and intended that these tombs should stay sound and dry for all eternity, and they probably would have done so if it were not for the ravages of man.

Gold was first discovered in the Wicklow Mountains around 2000 B.C.E. (the early Bronze Age—when the Minoans were constructing their magnificent Temple of Cnossus on Crete, and the Mycenaeans were settling mainland Greece). The ancient Irish began making beautiful gold ornaments and necklaces soon to be in great demand in the markets throughout Europe. This generated another migration, and the last prehistoric invasion of Ireland, which lasted from approximately 2000 to approximately 1200 B.C.E.

The first of these people were known as the "Beaker Folk" (named for their style of pottery). They were a round-headed race from the great Indo-European family that developed into the various Celtic tribes. This was truly the beginning of Celtic Ireland, and these invaders developed into an extraordinarily tough, spirited, and mystical race of people. Most all present-day Europeans, Middle Easterners, and Indian peoples are descendents of the Celtic branch of this Indo-European family, according to most researchers. Their ancestors were the Ur people from the regions of the Volga Steppes in what is currently western Russia. They were among the first to domesticate the horse, and when they rode them into Thessaly around 3000 B.C.E., looking extremely terrifying and powerful, they gave rise to the legends of the Centaurs. They occupied Greece, Persia and parts of India until approximately 1750 B.C.E. They were also the founders of the Hittite Empire in Anatolia (modern-day Turkey and northern Syria), who became a great power from 1400 to 1200 B.C.E., and are mentioned in the Jewish Torah, and the Christian Old Testament Biblical Scriptures.

In reference to Ireland, and contrary to much current popular belief, the Celtic people were not a pure bloodline by any means. They were a blend of many peoples, some warriors, some traders, many were farmers, who intermarried and settled out together. They developed distinct communities based on a common language, customs, occupations, religion, and identity. They assimilated more readily in Ireland with the native peoples than they did on the continent. Far more! There are several researchers today who claim the widely ranging Celts should not even be spoken of as a race at all, but were quite diverse groups from very different bloodlines.

The use of iron, brought into westernmost Europe from the area of the Caucasus (between the Caspian and Black Seas), entered the culture of the Celtic peoples from between 1100 and 900 B.C.E. This made the Celts, who were already fierce and extremely feared warriors, even that much more devastating, and by the beginning of the Third Century B.C.E., they had become Europe's most dominant power—their power and sphere of influence extended from present-day Italy, Portugal, and Spain in the South; to Rumania, Yugoslavia, and Bulgaria in the East; and, through most of what is now Germany, France, Switzerland, and the British Isles in the North and West.

This continental period of Celtic ascendancy is known as the "La Tene" period, named for one of the earliest archaeological sites found in Switzerland. This culture featured accomplishments that were far superior to anything known to date. In this hierarchical society, the aristocratic warriors shared the highest social positions with the Kings and the Druids, who were a combination priest, philosopher, historian, prophet, astronomer, teacher, judge, and poet. Artists and artisans were ranked only slightly lower in this social hierarchy. The particular Celtic peoples that migrated to Ireland were mostly from groups known as the Milesians and the Gaels, with the Gaels eventually gaining dominance over most of the island.

The Celts never much attempted to develop a written language, although they did possess one. It was known as Ogham (from Ogma the god of words), and was reproduced by carving into stones (known as Ogham stones), many of which may still be seen throughout Ireland (there is one fantastic example within the church ruins at Ardmore monastery in County Waterford. Evidently the monks brought it in and housed it in a niche within the nave, hence preserving it far more efficiently than most). The Druids were the most knowledgeable within these early societies, and wished to only transmit their knowledge orally, to personally selected or chosen individuals. They could have easily recorded it, but chose not to do so, claiming it would lose much of its magic and power if this was done.

The Celtic peoples also constructed no temples—their religious rituals were performed outdoors in a grove of oak trees, which were considered sacred to the Celts. Their faith was also far more complex than anything yet known. They had moved from worshipping the objects of nature (the rocks, rivers, mountains, etc.) to worshipping the forces of nature (the sun, the sea, the moon, and the wind). This was extremely advanced at the time. After these deities they had a pantheon of lesser gods that governed every aspect of human life, such as fertility, agriculture, commerce, war, etc. These gods corresponded very closely to the pantheon of Greek, Roman (who pretty much copied the Greeks), and Norse gods. Remember—it is believed all these came from a common Indo-European ancestry as well.

The Celts believed the human spirit was immortal, they believed in reincarnation, and they believed that the human spirit could travel throughout life in a variety of forms. Music and poetry facilitated these travels and were practiced as being divine. Eloquence was as valued as bravery in battle, and a well-spoken poet could calm the most insanely enraged warrior. Diodorus Siculus, a first century Greek historian, wrote that when two armies faced off against one another, with weapons drawn and tempers at a fever's pitch, the poets would often throw themselves into the middle of the fracas and restore calm—as if they were taming savage beasts. Quite often, even among the most vicious barbarians, anger would submit to wisdom; and, the god of war would pay homage to that of the muses, and submit completely if the argument was articulate, truthful, and sound enough.

The art of the Celts was extremely elegant and sophisticated, and in great demand throughout the known world. They had learned enameling from the people of the east. They elaborately ornamented most all leather, wood, metal, and stone utensils, artifacts, and weaponry. They also learned the art of coloring glass, probably from the early Phoenicians. They were great weavers and dyers of fabric as well.

Ancient Celtic stones aligned to identify the reef for sailors.

The Celtic kings were generally great patrons of the arts, and from approximately 600 A.D. onward, so was the early Irish Christian Church. This combination produced what is known as the "Golden Age" in Ireland. Many incredibly elaborate and ornate artifacts have come to us from this period, most notably the Tara Brooch, the Ardagh Chalice, the Moylough Belt-Shrine, the Derrynaflan Hoard, the beautiful High Crosses incorporating both Celtic and Christian motifs; and, perhaps most importantly, the great illuminated manuscripts such as the Book of Durrow, the Book of Kells, the Book of Armagh, and so forth. A good many of these artifacts and the elaborate gold work may be seen in the National Museum of Ireland, located on Kildare Street in Dublin. It is possibly interesting to note that most everywhere in the world, the various "golden ages" were generally ended by barbarians, or should we say peoples of substantially less sophistication, and this also became the case in Ireland when the Norse, or Vikings, began invading from around 795 or so.

The Celts as mentioned were superb craftsmen and woodworkers, building some of the first chariots. They invented the bucket and barrel made from wood (usually oak), and these soon replaced pottery in northern Europe. They invented the scythe and rotary grain mill (two major agricultural advancements).

The Celts valued education as highly as fierce warfare, and one would study at the school of a Druid for more than twenty years to attain knowledge in philosophy, astronomy, law, religion, geography, history, and more. As previously mentioned, all teaching was oral and cast in verse, or rhyme—poetic in nature, for easy memorization. These were the origins of the great Irish poetry tradition, and in fact the Irish druids, poets, and bards introduced rhyme to the world, as prior to Druidic verse all previous verse throughout Europe was in the form of alliteration only.

In spite of all this, the continental Celts especially were primarily known as extremely fierce and savage warriors. They were large people, with fair hair and skin, and were terrifying to the small dark people of southern Europe. Even more terrifying was their method of fighting, presenting a wild and furious onslaught of horsemen, chariots, and warriors. They would scream at the top of their lungs, this accompanied by the discordant blowing of horns, and the rhythmic beating of swords against their shields. The tales claim that before going into battle they would dance wildly and leap around until worked into a frenzy, shouting insults and threats, and then many of them would rip off all their armor, helmets, and clothing, rushing into battle completely naked, and with no fear whatsoever. One can only imagine the sight of this.

After the battle they would engage in elaborate feasts where huge amounts of food, wine, and mead were consumed (mead was an alcoholic beverage made from fermented honey. A supply meant to last for the cycle of one full moon was also traditionally given to newlyweds as they went into seclusion, and is the origin of the term "honeymoon"). Poets and bards would then tell of the warriors' exploits in the battles, as well as those of their ancestors. Another terrifying practice of certain Celts was that of cutting off the heads of their defeated opponents, and then tying them to the necks of their horses. Later they would embalm them with cedar oil and display them on the walls of their homes. Lucan, the Roman poet, wrote that death meant nothing to the Celts, as their spirits would immediately take another body, and even at times re-inhabit the same one.

This is for certain the generally accepted perception of the Celts, but it must be noted that this stereotype is far more applicable to the European Celts than it is to the Irish Celts. They were a much more subdued people and the Irish Celtic wars were generally not near as violent and basically consisted of small skirmishes lasting perhaps a couple of hours, at the outside a day or two, usually simply a raid to steal cattle or an effort to recover an unpaid debt. "One might almost argue that cattle-raiding was a cleverly enacted national sport during the Golden Period of the Irish Celts (400-800 A.D.)", stated Etienne Rynne of the Department of Archaeology, University College, Galway. A man's wealth and status were based on cattle ownership. Coinage as a monetary exchange was not used in Ireland until the sixteenth century.

The Irish weapons at this time were really rather primitive compared to elsewhere. The only weapons used during the Irish Celtic ascendancy seem to have been a small sword, the spear, and the javelin; but they were quite proficient with these, especially the spear and the javelin. After the fall of Rome, the Irish made several raids into Britain and Wales, winning many battles and establishing numerous colonies, including many of those in what was later to become Scotland.

The Irish Celts were an outdoors people, understanding and worshipping all aspects of nature. The oak trees were sacred, as was water and the natural springs, most of which became holy wells after the coming of Christianity. They never built any towns. They never attempted to form a centralized working government or empire, although their numbers and sphere of influence were certainly vast enough to do so.

The European Celts defeated the Romans and sacked Rome first in 390 B.C.E. (something the Romans never forgot). In fact, the Romans were so traumatized that they deemed this occurrence year one of their calendar and designated this as the very beginning of Roman history. The great Roman legions of the era of Julius Caesar and Caesar Augustus held them in check for a couple of hundred years. Julius Caesar himself compiled a rather lengthy journal and wrote often about the Celts and a wee bit about the Druids. He also dramatically reduced their numbers and drove them from Gaul in 51 B.C.E.

The Romans however, never got to Ireland (at least as soldiers—many came later to Ireland and studied at the great monasteries). Neither did the Angles, Saxons, Jutes, Frisians, Lombards, Huns, Vandals, Goths, Franks, Merovingians, nor any other of the western European migrating barbarians ever reach Ireland. In fact each time the aforementioned groups came to power it more or less had the affect of isolating Ireland from the rest of the European continent, and the Celtic influenced culture remained intact in Ireland for well over two thousand years with only relatively minor changes, until it was transformed into something of unique spiritual and scholarly genius by the coming of Christianity in the fourth century. In fact Ireland, the Isle of Man, and a few isolated areas in the Highlands of current Scotland, are the only places that can claim a much longer influence from the Celtic cultures and heritage than elsewhere in Europe. These pockets for the most part remained untouched until the coming of the Norse and Danes (or Vikings), in the eighth and ninth centuries; and, in Ireland these Celts were different politically, socially, linguistically, and artistically from all the others, and this remained so far longer than anywhere else.

The Irish Celts were in fact, as previously mentioned, a very spiritual and mystical people; and, there seems to be a great resurgence of interest today among academics in the Celtic ways, and especially in the ways and activities of the Druids, who, in addition to all the other functions previously mentioned, were also prophets and/or soothsayers (the Druids, according to ancient writings, foretold the comings of both St. Patrick and St. Colmcille).

The Druids were also in charge of the annual festivals, which were based on the heavens and the agricultural cycle. In Ireland there were generally four major festivals:

Imbolc—the feast of renewal and purification celebrated on February 1. It was dedicated to the pagan Goddess Brigit, whom after the advent of Christianity sort of blended together with St. Brigit of Kildare.

Beltaine—a feast asking for a bountiful harvest and for good weather during the growing season. It was celebrated on May 1, and was one of the important "fire festivals". It was the forerunner of May Day, an important springtime festival celebrated in the Americas and elsewhere until the latter half of the twentieth century.

Lughnasa—the feast of fertility and first fruits. It was celebrated on August 1, and was dedicated to the harvest and the hunt to supply winter food. (Lughnasa is also the Irish word for the month of August).

Samhain—a festival dedicated to all the gods and the Celtic spirits of the "otherworld". It is the 3000 year old forerunner of our present-day Halloween. It commemorated the creation of the world and the transformation of chaos into order. On that night all supernatural entities, including the spirits of our ancestral dead, returned to wander among the living, thus imposing great danger as they hoped to avenge the wrongs that had been done to them. It was customary to put food outside the homes in an effort to appease the spirits who wanted to come back into the homes, eat and warm themselves by the family hearth, and then eventually avenge the wrongs done them. It was celebrated on October 31, and was renamed "All Saints' Day", and then "All Hallows' Eve", following the advent of Christianity, before finally becoming "Halloween".

It was also known as the "fire festival of the dead", as all old fires had to be extinguished and then ceremonially relit from a sacred fire that was tended only by the Druids.

There was one main annual local gathering or festival known as "oenach", or the festival of the tuath. It was presided over by the king (or Ri) and at this festival he would confirm all laws and treaties adopted by the tuath, perform marriages, settle lawsuits, and collect taxes. The members of the tuath would participate in games and trade. It would end with a mystic spiritual ceremony led by the Druids.

The Druids were mentioned by Aristotle in the Fourth Century B.C.E. and, as mentioned previously, were written about in the First Century B.C.E. by

Julius Caesar, who wrote, "The Druids officiate at the worship of the gods, regulate public and private sacrifices, and give rulings on all religious questions. Large numbers of young men flock to them for instruction, and they are held in great honor by the people. They act as judges in practically all disputes, whether between tribes or between individuals". Cicero, the Roman historian also writing at the turn of the First/Second Centuries B.C.E. noted the Druids "had great knowledge of physics and astronomy"; and, the Roman historian, Pliny, wrote in the First Century C.E. (A.D.) that they were responsible for preserving medical knowledge. The extremely well preserved body of a 2000 year old Celt, found in a bog near Manchester, England, in the Twentieth Century, known to archaeology as "Lindow Man", is believed by many to be that of a Druid, primarily because of body markings, grave contents, and especially because of its unusually smooth hands.

There are two main theories regarding the origin of the word "Druid", both based on the ancient Indo-European language known as Sanskrit. The Sanskrit word for oak tree is "druh", and the Greek word for oak tree is "drus", and because the Druids revered the oak tree, it is deducted this is the origin of the word. The other theory simply goes one step further and combines the word "druh" with another Indo-European word "wid", which means "wisdom" or "to know".

As mentioned, the Celts of Ireland retained their culture far longer than their counterparts in continental Europe, with perhaps recognizable remnants even remaining in Ireland to this very day. The impetus for Celtic change, and the next major influence on the island, was Christianity. The Celts took to Christianity quite readily as they had long believed in persons of great faith and discipline being able to move back and forth from the human to the spiritual world. They also believed in the future coming of a great human god—a savior if you will. They also had no problem with angels, as they had long believed in spirits with similar responsibilities—through English translation and literary interpretation today these spirits are called faeries or even ghosts; but, when considering the original oral folklore tales and stories (as we know them) they sound very much the same as Christian angels. Many scholars have proposed that the early Celtic Spirituality was quite possibly the purest form of Christianity the world has yet known.

In Ireland, the period just prior to the coming of Christianity is known as the "Heroic Period". Our main source of information regarding the Heroic Period comes to us through a series of tales known as the "Ulster Cycle". The stories of the Ulster Cycle were perpetuated through the centuries orally by the Druids, poets (filidh in Irish), and bards. (As mentioned, these were the three most prestigious and learned positions in Celtic society. These individuals could all facilitate movement between this world and the otherworld (spiritual world). The bards accomplished this through eulogies and satires as well as through musical compositions and were a major contributor to the mystical and magical effects produced in Celtic feasting rituals. Bardic schools were a major educational resource and remained active well after Celtic times and even into the Middle Ages. In fact there is still today a Bardic School active in Ireland known as The National Eisteddford Association, founded in 1880.) The "Ulster Cycle" stories were then later written and recorded by Christian monks, who were extremely fascinated by the pagan Celtic folktales and religious beliefs.

The Ulster Cycle stories deal with customs, great feats and journeys, love stories, kings and rulers, heroes, and of course wars (the tragic focus of far too many human stories). Here we first learn of King Conchobar of Ulster and his Red Branch Knights, who were ruthless and constantly at war with the rest of Ireland, especially Connacht, who was led by King Ailill and his fiercely combative wife Queen Maeve, who lived near what is presently Rathcroghan in County Roscommon. This was in the First Century—approximately 2000 years ago—rather interesting eh?

The most famous of the Ulster Cycle stories is an extremely lengthy epic poem entitled the "Tain Bo Cuailnge" (translated as the "Cattle Raid of Cooley") and relates the exploits of the great warrior hero Cuchulain (a beautiful statue of whom now graces the lobby of the General Post Office on O'Connell Street in Dublin). Cuchulain embodied all the cherished ideals of the Irish Celts—He was the perfect Warrior/Aristocrat, full of courage, loyalty, truth, physical beauty, honor, deep respect for women, extreme arrogance, and a nonchalant disregard for death. He leaves no descendents (he kills his only son unknowingly in a tragic duel). He is indestructible on the field of battle, an eternal youth, who is only conquered in the end by the deception of magic. Other stories deal with a tragic female hero, Deirdre, who retains her spirit while fighting against all odds. No one now knows for certain how much of these tales are fact and how much is myth—but many of the major facts have been substantiated elsewhere—such as the names, locations and exploits of certain of the Celtic kings and so forth.

The Fenian Cycle, or Fenian traditions, came along approximately three hundred years after the Ulster Cycle. Although paganism is still incorporated, it is modified or subdued somewhat. Christianity is represented as coming along late in the life of the Fenian's most famous poet, Ossian (these stories have also been often referred to as the "Ossianic Cycle"). These stories are much less violent, dealing less with war and death, and more with the beauty of nature and romance. The great hero of the Fenian Cycle is Fionn mac Cumhaill (popularly anglicized as Finn McCool) and the primary method of delivery is the ballad. The stories revolve around two feuding clans (or Tuaths), the Clan Baoisgne and the Clan Morna. The king of Clan Baoisgne was killed, but his wife then gave birth to a secret son by the name of Demna, later called Fionn (meaning "fair child"). He was raised in a forest to protect him from the Clan Morna and would grow to lead his clan in an effort to avenge his father's death and to claim his inheritance. The Fenian Cycle begins with the lengthy epic *Acallam na Senorech* (translated as *The Colloquy of the Old Men*) written circa 1200. The greatest prose story of the era is *Toraigheacht Agus Ghrainne* (*The Pursuit of Diarmuid and Grainne*), something of a reworking of the Ulster Cycle stories about Deirdre. Fionn's exploits begin with a story entitled "Fionn and the Salmon".

The Ulster Cycle stories, with the exception of the few mentioned, have been for the most part lost and forgotten. Many of the Fenian stories on the other hand remain with us to this very day. Geoffrey of Monmouth and Chretien des Troyes, the two authors responsible for the tales of King Arthur and the Knights of the Round Table, Camelot, Sir Lancelot, and all of that both acknowledged that their stories were in a large part based on those of the Fenian Cycle. The Arthurian legends were the main literary works read all through the middle ages, and greatly influenced medieval life with their tales of romance, errant knights, doomed lovers, visions, voyages, and adventures throughout an earthly paradise.

The kings ruled over "Tuaths", which were collections of families and may well be translated as "communities". A family was called a "fine" and legally consisted of all relation in the male line of descent for five generations. The Tuaths were the ruling forces in pagan Ireland. There were from 100 to 300 Tuaths in Ireland when Christianity arrived. The term "Tuath" also referred to the land each occupied. The royal family was known as the "derb-fine". The term "celi" referred to the commoners, or "clients", or perhaps "vassals" or farmers.

The Tuaths were grouped into five over-kingdoms—Ulster, Connacht, Leinster, Munster, and Tara, each ruled by an Overking called the "Ard-Ri". The Overkings were elected, not selected by birth, and theoretically must be flawless—morally, socially, physically, and many were considered by the people to be descended from the gods, or at least in communication with the gods. Regional kingdoms were established by a number of tuatha joining together in alliances for the purposes of defense and trade.

Dagda (meaning the "good") was the main god of the Irish Celts (He was called "Sucellos" in Celtic Gaul). His son was "Ogma" (the "honey-mouthed"). He was the god of learning, and later, literature. Ogma's followers were the "filidh" (the poets), and these went all the way back to the legendary beginning of Ireland, when Amergin, a Druid and the son of Mil, chanted a poetic incantation to the beings of earth and sky, when he first came to the Irish shore. The Irish Celts had developed an alphabet and system of writing known as "Ogham" (after the god, Ogma), but it was difficult and cumbersome and was completely discarded with the arrival of Latin and the Roman alphabet, which made writing so much easier.

The sorcery of words was only equaled by the spell of music, which was bequeathed to the Irish Celts by the god, "Lug", who had received this gift from Dagda, who comforted his wife, Boann (namesake of the River Boyne), with music during childbirth. Music is of course still extremely important and mystical to the Irish. The national symbol is Dagda's Harp, and the Harper held the next most prestigious social position following that of Poet. (By the way, many of the oldest Irish settlements and inhabitants were located along the River Boyne, with their origins being uncertain—perhaps settlements of the gods?)

The Irish Celts also had a deeply sensuous respect for the ways and pleasures of nature, as well as a great fondness for animals. The horse was the Celtic passion and is still an Irish passion yet today. I don't believe that anywhere on earth does horse racing hold more status, and the annual Galway Races are the richest on earth, drawing competitors from every continent. (According to the Ulster Cycle legend, Cuchulain's horse, the Gray of Macha, held him up during his final battle and supplied him with blood until they both died together.) The Irish Celts were renowned for their domestication of the great "Wolf-Dogs", which were in high demand throughout Europe and were presented to kings as presents. When seven of them were brought to Rome during the Fourth Century, they terrified all who saw them.

The impact of this love of nature was at an all-time high during the Fenian Cycle era of Finn MacCumail and his son, Ossian the poet. His stories form the Ossianic (or Fenian) Cycle and as mentioned previously came just after the Ulster Cycle, and the Heroic Age—the late second and third centuries. They talk of a deep ascetic love of nature—the song of a bird, the color of the morning sky, the falling of leaves, etc. Trees of the forest were protected by law and assigned various ranks, with the oak tree at the top and considered sacred. Finn's followers, the Fianna, lived solitary lives on the fringes of society, and surely laid the groundwork for the great Irish Monastic movement soon to follow. One of Finn's wives was a doe deer, and Finn could change into a deer whenever he so desired. The Irish Celts were extremely knowledgeable regarding natural herbs and medicinal botany. This they also passed along to the Irish monks, claiming they had received this information from the gods.

Other Celtic gods worth noting would include "Manannan", the god of the sea. He came from what is now known as the Isle of Man (named for him). He was a seaman who could look to the heavens and know whether the seas would be calm or stormy. Brigit, Anu, and Dana were goddesses of fertility and prosperity. Anu and Dana were the mothers of the gods, and Brigit watched over childbirth, bringing prosperity to the homes she visited, leaving her footprints in the ashes of the hearth. She was also the goddess of poetry. Maeve was the goddess of war and sovereignty. She was the namesake of the famous Connacht queen, but was worshipped in Ireland centuries before the Heroic Age. Every King of Tara married her symbolically. She was the Queen-Wolf who could outrun a horse, and her lover was Fergus, who ate seven times as much as any other man, had the strength of seven-hundred men; and, his nose, mouth, and penis were each seven fingers long. His scrotum was as large as a sack of flour, and when Maeve was away, he needed seven women to comfort him. Welcome Christianity!

Christianity, Irish Saints and Monasticism

As we know, Christianity was heavily persecuted on the continent and elsewhere until the coming of the Roman Emperor Constantine, and his issuance of the Edict of Milan in 313 C.E. (A.D.), guaranteeing religious toleration for Christians. Earlier Roman Emperors saw Christianity as dangerously revolutionary and tried fervently to eradicate it. Christians were blamed for all natural disasters and military defeats because it was believed they angered the gods. Persecutions became most vicious under the Emperors Decius and Valerian in the third century but the last desperate, and surely the most ruthless effort, was attempted by Diocletian in 303, decreeing that Christians were not citizens and could not own property. He confiscated all Christian property, destroyed the churches, imprisoned the clergy, burned all sacred books, then enslaved and killed Christians by the hundreds (very similar to what the British would later do to the Irish Catholics).

Until the time of Constantine, Christianity was practiced in virtual secrecy, perpetuated mostly by the hermit ascetic monks living in the deserts of Egypt, Syria, and Judea. Under the influence of Constantine, Christianity flourished and spread like never before, and after the fall of Rome to the Christianized Alaric, the Visigoths, and the Ostrogoths in 453, the impetus for the growth of Christianity moved further north and west. This isolated ascetic monastic lifestyle was ideally suited to the ways of the Irish Celts.

A brief history examining some of the early monastic movements may help to clarify this concept. Saint Antony of Egypt is considered to be the father of hermit monasticism. He was born in Alexandria around 250 C.E. Pachomius, a former general under Constantine, organized ascetic monks into the first structured communities, made them economically self sufficient, subjected them to certain rules; and, by the time of his death in 346, had established nine monasteries with over three-thousand monks, as well as the first monastery for women.

Saint Basil of Cappadocia (present-day central Turkey) then declared that monasteries should be of service to the community and established almshouses, schools, and hospitals at his monasteries; and, a rule (guidelines) for monasteries that became the model adhered to by most monasteries all through the Middle Ages, and is yet today the model for monasteries of the Greek and Slavonic churches.

The great organizer of western monasticism is considered to be Saint Benedict of Nursia (c.480-547), but by his time there were several monasteries already established in Ireland, as we shall see. Saint Benedict also wrote one of the early rules for monasteries entitled "The Little Rule for Beginners". In this he outlined specific organizational rules relevant to monastic life. In the rule of Saint Benedict, manual labor and prayer were the main focus, the Benedictine motto being "Ora et Labora" (a bit later on manual labor was defined to include academic labors as well). One extremely important new revolutionary concept expounded was that each monk must swear an oath of stability, uniting him forever to the particular monastery at which he took his vows (this became an extremely important concept for various monastic orders over the years). He also promoted that cenobitic (religious) life should be lived under the direction of an abbot at each monastery whose word was supreme; and, St. Benedict's rule adhered to exclusively. The abbots or founders of most the early Irish monasteries were considered to be Catholic Bishops.

Celtic (pagan) Ireland had no cities. The monasteries became the first "cities", and centers of education, spirituality, social life, and public welfare. In Ireland, all religious life was centered in, and revolved around, the monasteries—not the diocesan bishoprics and cathedrals, as was the case on the continent. (Note: It is quite possible that in many areas of the world yet today, as well as in the future, the monastic setting may again prove to be the most efficient and beneficial lifestyle, offering a superior education, compassionate and affordable health care, concerned social programs, serious spiritual study, etc.)

Saint Benedict's rule was first brought to Britain in 597, by Saint Augustine, who had been sent by Pope Gregory I "Gregory the Great" (both were Benedictines) to both preach to, and of course convert, the Saxons who had just taken control of the island. Following the Synod of Whitby in 664 (called to settle differences between the Roman church and the Irish, or Celtic, church), the Benedictine rule was the rule used by the vast majority of the monasteries in Britain up until 1540-1555, when agents of Henry VIII dissolved and looted all the monasteries.

I'm getting a bit ahead of the story here, we must go back to the fourth century and the influence of those first ascetic desert monastics, Saint Antony, Saint Pachomius, and Saint Basil. Disciples of these had moved into Wales, Cornwall, Gaul, and Italy by the end of the fourth century, establishing monasteries, schools, and almshouses in an attempt to Christianize the pagan Celts.

Two of the most notable of these, and the two who may have most arguably influenced Christianity the most in Ireland, were St. Ninnian of Whithorn and St. Martin of Tours. Both of these founded monasteries—St. Ninnian in the northern land of the Britons and St. Martin in Gaul (modern-day France). St. Martin of Tours some believe may have been a maternal uncle of St. Patrick.

Many people mistakenly believe that St. Patrick first brought Christianity to Ireland, when he returned the second time in the mid Fifth Century. There is substantial evidence to indicate that Christianity was known and practiced in Ireland by the end of the First Century. There are ancient writings that even claim the apostles James and Paul both visited Ireland in the First Century.

A Spanish Historian, Julian of Toledo, writing at the end of the First Century claims that St. James, addressed a letter from Ireland To the Spanish Jewish Community, and Vincentius of Bauvais stated that, "James, the son of Zebedee, preached in Ireland, and when he returned to Jersusalem, where he was martyred, had with him seven Irish disciples."

The writings of the Historians, Eusebius and Nichephorus, also claimed that these apostles visited Ireland and the western islands. They also wrote of several Irishmen, among them Conal Cearnach, who went to Jerusalem, were baptized, and took the faith back to Ireland and especially back to one, Conor MacNessa, probably a local king.

We know that the Roman Legions also brought Christianity to Britain from the First Century onward. At the Council of Arles in 314, we know there were Bishops from Britain in attendance. The Historian, Bollandus, writes that Palladius, who was sent by Rome to Ireland a short time before Patrick, and given the mission of converting the Irish, "probably found more Christians already there than he ever converted". He only stayed seven months, founded three churches quickly according to his own account, none of which have any remaining evidence, and left the island. He did not get along with the Irish, and went to Alba (Scotland) where he founded a monastery and died only a few years later.

There is a good body of evidence that Irish Christians played a prominent role on the Continent well before the time of Patrick—several had gained considerable literary and ecclesiastical eminence. One of those most notable was named Manseutus (or Mansuey)—He was sent by Rome to be the Bishop of Toul (in Lorraine—the province in Gaul—currently on the border of France and Belgium) nearly a century before Patrick.

St. Florentinus, according to the historians was Irish. St. Florentinus was imprisoned at the hands of the Roman Emperor Claudius. While in prison he supposedly converted and baptized ninety-six people, including his jailer, Asterius.

The Christian poet Sedulius (in Irish, Siadal) was said to be Irish and was the first to translate into Latin much of the poetry and Irish rhyme, which up until that time was only found in Ireland. He traveled extensively throughout southern Europe and Asia, and dedicated one of his works to the Roman Emperor Theodosius.

The most infamous of all these was a brilliant rhetorician named Celestius, a famous lawyer in Rome, and disciple of Pelagius (who argued fervently his heretical doctrines regarding the divinity of Christ about forty or fifty years before Patrick came to Ireland. St. Jerome wrote of him often, abusing him vigorously). Celestius later went to Carthage and preached against St. Augustine of Hippo. He also argued before the Patriarch in Constantinople and the Pope in Rome, being forcibly ejected from both these places according to historical accounts. Dr. Douglas Hyde, writing in his "A Literary History of Ireland" from 1899 also claimed that Pelagius himself was Irish.

A scripted "High Cross" from County Galway. Many of these crosses incorporate both Christian and Celtic motifs and were constructed from the fourth to the twelfth centuries. Hundreds of these stone crosses are to be found throughout the Irish countryside, as they have been far better preserved than most anywhere else, due in part to Ireland's historical isolation from the various barbarian types that ravaged the European continent.

Irish-Christian influence on the continent has been well established, and Irish historians are also in agreement that there were at least four of the Irish Saints active in Ireland before the arrival of Patrick—These were St. Declan of Ardmore, St. Ailbe of Emly, St. Ibar of Beg Erin, and St. Ciaran of Saighir and Ossory; and, we've already mentioned Palladius as well, who landed in County Wicklow, stayed only a short time, and then left (or was driven out by the Leinster Chieftain, Nathi)—there are various accounts.

I'll discuss a bit more about these Saints, but I don't wish in any way to diminish from the incredible impact of Patrick's coming to Ireland. It was an epoch of immense proportions, not only for Ireland but for the entire Christian world as well.

Saint Declan was of the tribe, or clan, known as the Deisi, a very powerful Celtic people who had moved from the north to settle in Munster. He was descended from the Kings of Tara. As with all the Irish Saints, and Scholars, there are many stories associated with him and his exploits. It is said there was a ball of fire seen above the house when Declan was born, and as his mother lifted him up, his head struck a stone. Declan was not hurt, but the stone retained the image of his head, and when it rained, the water collected in this indented area, and this rain water would cure all sickness. As a young man, it is reported he exhibited neither faults nor ill desires. When he went to Rome to continue his studies, he was ordained a Bishop by the Pope and sent back to Ireland to preach and convert. Over fifty Romans returned with him, including Runan, the son of the King of Rome, with whom he was a close friend and whom he held quite dear. It is said that he also met Ailbe in Rome and they formed a close friendship that lasted all their lives. Another story claims that he met Patrick on the road as he was leaving Rome.

Perhaps his most famous story relates that when Declan and his entourage reached the European coast, they had no money and could find no boat to transport them. Declan had been given a little black bell by God for use only in emergencies. He rang the bell and an empty ship appeared with no sails. It carried them to Ireland and then vanished. The bell however was accidentally left behind. An extremely distressed Declan asked God for help and the entire rock upon which the bell was left floated across the sea and came to rest on the coast of County Waterford. The rock is supposedly still there with a hole in it, which according to the legend was burned into it by the bell; and, as the story goes, only people without sin can pass through the hole.

It is said that several priests and bishops have tried to have this object of superstition removed, but have never been able to find workmen that would perform this act of believed sacrilege, as the love of St. Declan remains that strong in the area yet today. Declan built his monastery and church where this rock came to rest and called the place Ardmore (meaning "Great Hill"). This land for the monastery and church had been given to Declan by the king of the Deisi. Declan as I mentioned was greatly loved for his founding of several churches throughout the area; and, according to legend converted more pagans than could be counted. When St. Ailbe was near death, it is told he came and spent the last fourteen days of his life at Ardmore, where the two Saints engaged in peaceful contemplation and prayer.

It is also written that Declan visited St. David, the Patron Saint of Wales, who was also of the Deisi clan, but if this is accurate it would mean that Declan lived nearly two-hundred years, as Declan was also reported to be present when St. Patrick converted King Aengus of Munster at the Rock of Cashel, over a hundred years before David was even born. Hence it is not likely all of the stories are completely accurate.

Throughout history, Ardmore, which is located right on the coast, has at times been an island, and at times a part of the mainland. It is currently part of the mainland, but certain experts claim it will soon again become an island. At Ardmore there is a great round tower and a stone cathedral with beautiful ancient carvings, as well as a small stone house where it is said Declan's remains are entombed, St. Declan's Oratory. The Celtic Sea is quite wild and turbulent throughout this area, but it is remarkably calm and placid here at Ardmore.

As was mentioned, it is reported Declan met Ailbe in Rome and the two became lifetime friends. Saint Ailbe is said to have lived 167 years, from 360 until 527. This may in fact be true, but it is more likely that this is a composite of himself and perhaps one of his followers who possibly assumed the same name, which was a custom among some at the time. Remember the accounts of these early Saints were not recorded until years later by the Christian Monks—and then only from the oral accounts passed down through the years.

As the story goes Ailbe was born to a Maidservant in the House of Cronan, Lord of Eliach, in County Tipperary. Cronan was very upset by the birth of the illegitimate child and ordered that the baby be thrown to the dogs, wolves, and wild beasts, so that he may be devoured. The Baby was protected by one of the wolves, guarding him and tending to him for three days until he was found by a Christian passing by. The Christian then took him away and raised him in the faith. Ailbe eventually studied in Rome, was ordained and sent back to Ireland by the Pope to preach and convert, along with at least twelve recently converted Irishmen.

They landed first in Northern Ireland where he converted the King, Fintan, and brought back to life three of Fintan's sons who had been killed in battle. He traveled throughout Ireland preaching until he finally settled out near his boyhood home at Emly, County Tipperary. There he built a church and school and wrote the "Rule of Ailbe", supposedly the first codification of ecclesiastical Rule in Ireland. He met Patrick at Cashel, which is just down the road, who reportedly named him Archbishop of Munster. He was greatly loved and adored, especially by Aengus, King of Munster whom Patrick converted. Ailbe supposedly wanted to go to Tyle (present-day Iceland) to retire and die, but Aengus wouldn't permit him to go because of his, and the people of Munster's, great love for Ailbe.

Relatively little is known of Saint Ibar—he was probably born in Ulster of royal lineage but the main focus of his activity was in County Wexford, where he built a monastery at Beg Erin, an island in Wexford Harbor (It is also no longer an island). Over 150 Monks lived at the Monastery and his school attracted scholars from all over Ireland and the European continent—most of these were probably Gaulish Scholars fleeing the invasion of the Huns—Ireland was already becoming a sanctuary for Scholars and Holy Men by the end of the fourth century.

The monastery on Inishmurray was founded by St. Molaise in the sixth century (A wooden statue of him was found there and is now in the National Museum of Ireland in Dublin). Inishmurray is one of the best preserved monastic sites on earth due primarily to the fact accessibility is quite difficult. It is located approximately an hour off the coast of County Sligo and the seas are so turbulent there that it is possible to disembark onto the island only a few days per year. There is also archaeological evidence that Neolithic peoples once inhabited the island. The last inhabitants to leave did so in 1948, after the island had been used for several centuries as a location for making some of Ireland's best poteen.

Inishmurray. The beehive huts of the monks were generally built over a depression in the soil, with lintel stones and then sea stones stacked above. A large slab of rock was taken inside and used as a bed. Other rocks served as tables and shelves.

Saint Ciaran was born in approximately 375 C.E. on Clear Island County Cork. This is a rather small island in the southernmost part of Ireland. It was home to only a couple hundred people. When he was about seven years old, it is told he brought back to life a bird that had fallen from a tree. He was baptized at the age of thirty, still in a state of grace and then went to Rome to study. He returned to Ireland and founded a church at the present site of the city of Kilkenny, County Kilkenny. The Kilkenny area was at that time only inhabited by wild animals and Ciaran's first disciples were a fox, a wolf, a deer and a badger. A Wild Boar at first resisted Ciaran but then later returned to be tamed. It then cut the materials with its tusks to build Ciaran's first dwelling. He lived alone until the word of his holiness reached the people, and converts were attracted to what was probably Ireland's First Monastery.

These four set the stage for the arrival of Saint Patrick. It is very difficult to separate myth from fact regarding the life of Patrick, as the stories took on a life of there own over the centuries following his death; but, some things are known for certain. He was a Celt, and not originally Irish (for this reason it is told he was not immediately embraced by some of these other Clerics we've just mentioned, especially Ibar) and the experts disagree as to the exact location of his birth. The theories range from the northernmost province of Celtic Briton, to the area that is now Wales, to the area of Brittany (in present-day France). In his Confessions, there is evidence to argue each of these locations as he simply names a town.

More and more experts seem to be of the belief that the continental origin may be correct, because it was from that region that he was taken captive at the age of sixteen. Also, St. Martin of Tours, as was previously mentioned, may have been his maternal uncle and lived in this region. Patrick's father was a Decurion (Magistrate) in the Roman Administration, and was probably a Christian. Patrick was born c. 390.

Little is known about Patrick's early years, up until the time he was captured and taken hostage at the age of sixteen by an Irish raiding party under the direction of Niall of the Nine Hostages, King of Ulster. He was then sold to a farmer named Milcho and forced to herd cattle on an extremely remote mountain, Slemish Mountain in County Antrim. He was totally isolated there, except for occasional contact with Irish Celts, and lived on roots and herbs; and, stated in his "Confession" that he came to pray often, saying over 100 prayers per day. He also came to love Ireland.

Boyle Abbey is located in the town of the same name in County Roscommon. It was built by the Cistercian monks in the Twelfth Century and served to house British troops for over three hundred years from the time of Queen Elizabeth I, at which time it was called Boyle Castle by the British.

Patrick learned the Irish language and was fascinated by the tales and fables of pagan Ireland. After six years of bondage, he one night had a vision that a ship was awaiting him on the coast. He escaped to the ship and after a year-and-a-half's journey finally made it back to his home. His family was overjoyed at his return and offered him land and livestock, but Patrick again had a vision in which he was handed letters from God charging him to become a priest and return to the pagan Irish. There was also a plea in one of the letters from the Irish begging him to return. He first went to Auxerre for study and was ordained a priest and then it is claimed he went to Rome where he was consecrated Bishop by Pope Celestine and commissioned to return to Ireland, although this has never been substantiated. It has for years been believed that he returned to Ireland in 432 A.D., with twenty-four companions, some being Irish Christians, but today several scholars believe it may have been a couple of decades later before he returned.

There are many stories regarding Patrick's exploits in Ireland, and as we've mentioned it is extremely difficult to separate fact from myth, but there are a few things of which we're relatively certain, and these include the fact he evidently traveled over most of the island; and, his philosophy was to convert the kings, as he knew all others would immediately follow, and he apparently converted several kings—including Dichu, whom was the first, in County Down. There are several different stories regarding the method in which the conversions were accomplished. For example Dichu supposedly set the wolf dogs on Patrick whom immediately turned them into stone. Dichu then raised his sword to strike Patrick and was unable to move his arm. He was according to accounts instantly converted.

Patrick then proceeded down the Boyne River Valley heading for Tara, the seat of the High-King of Ireland, who at that time was Laoghaire, son of Niall of the Nine Hostages, the one who had originally taken Patrick captive. Patrick arrived at the Hill of Slane, just across the Boyne River valley from the Hill of Tara, on the night before Easter, which also happened to be the eve of Beltaine (the Celtic fire festival of prayers, asking for a bountiful harvest and good weather).

The custom of the Celts was that on that night the Druids first lit a large fire to begin the prayers on the Hill of Tara. No other fires of any nature were to be lit before the Druids lit this fire. Well, Patrick lit a fire on the Hill of Slane, which immediately angered Laoghaire and the Druids, who then reminded Laoghaire that they had foretold this would happen, especially the most influential Druid, Matha Mac Umotr. He further reiterated that this was the fulfillment of that earlier prophetic vision and that the new fire lit would never be extinguished in Ireland.

Laoghaire then sent a party of warriors to either kill Patrick or bring him to Laoghaire early the next morning. Well, Patrick was already on the road to meet with Laoghaire, and had as we've mentioned learned the ways of the Celts. As he sensed the angry men approaching, he used the Druids own knowledge and when the warriors arrived they found only a herd of deer, with a fawn crying, and they passed right on by. It is said that Patrick at that time composed a hymn for God, called the Faed Fiada (The Deer's Cry) and he and his companions sang it on the road all the way to Tara. Some scholars claim this is the first hymn ever written in Irish Gaelic, and yet today the Irish sing it for protection.

As Patrick entered Laoghaire's encampment, the king's famous poet Dubthach and the King's favorite nobleman, Erc, rose in respect for Patrick-the first two converts at Tara. He was then confronted by the Druids who tried to confuse him with their magic, but Patrick's miracles were greater than theirs, including dispelling the darkness, the one thing the Druids could never accomplish. Most present were then converted, including Laoghaire. Other accounts state Laoghaire was not converted, but did allow Patrick to freely preach his faith.

There are numerous tales regarding Patrick's travels and preaching following Tara. It is known he traveled throughout County Meath and the province of Leinster, and then arrived in Connacht in 434. There he converted Laoghaire's two beautiful daughters, Ethni the Fair and Fedelm the Ruddy. He arrived at a place in County Mayo, now called Murrisk Abbey, as the season of Lent approached. It is at the foot of a steep mountain whose summit is in the clouds. Patrick decided to spend Lent high on the mountain fasting and praying in the extremely cold and windy conditions. He later said the entire time was spent in heavenly rapture. The mountain is now called Croagh Patrick and every year thousands make the pilgrimage to the top, most of them barefooted, as it is said Patrick was also.

Selskar Abbey located in Wexford town. It was built by Alexander de la Roche after returning from the Second Crusade to find his fiancé had become a Nun, after thinking he was dead. It was also the location where Henry II did his penance for the killing of Thomas a' Beckett at Canterbury.

As legend has it, before coming down Patrick ordered all the snakes and venomous creatures out of Ireland. The fact is, this tale was invented by Patrick's twelfth century biographer, Jocelyn, to add a sensational touch to the already huge mountain of impressive accomplishments attributed to Patrick. In truth, all the animals had been driven out during the ice age. When the glacial sheet receded, the rising waters covered the land bridges, first the one with Wales and a little later the one with Scotland before most of the animals could get back to Ireland, and after that none returned except those who could fly or swim. For over seven hundred years following Patrick's death this story regarding the snakes never existed. Jocelyn also devised the story of Patrick's converting the Irish by use of the shamrock to explain the Holy Trinity.

It is believed Patrick next went to Munster where he converted King Aengus at the Rock of Cashel. He then convened a Synod of Ireland at Cashel, and summoned the four Saints of the South we mentioned earlier, Ailbe, Ibar, Declan, and Ciaran.

Following his work in Munster, Patrick again headed north towards Ulster, passing through Leinster where he and King Laoghaire agreed he should restructure and codify the existing Brehon laws, the new code was called the Senchus Mor.

When he got to Ulster he founded the city of Armagh, built a monastery, a school, and a church. For the next several hundred years Armagh would be one of Europe's great centers of learning and religion. While at Armagh, Patrick wrote his "Confession" and "Epistle to Coroticus". Coroticus was a prince from Briton who made a raid into Ireland, killing and taking captive several hundred Irish—many of them Patrick's newly baptized converts. It's an intense document in which Patrick ironically condemns Briton's oppression, castigates Coroticus, and asks for the return of the hostages. The "Confession" of St. Patrick was a defense written in response to having a dear friend turn on him and report false accusations about his life and character.

Patrick passed away at Saul in County Down, the site of his first church, somewhere between the years 465 and 490, leaving behind a terribly grief-stricken people. His final years were spent in prayer and contemplation. The twelve days of his wake are known in Irish as "Laithi na Caointe" (the days of Lamentation). Patrick's impact on western civilization over the next several hundred years, and in reality up until today could never be measured. It has been said that he is to the Celtic and European peoples, what Confucius is to the Orientals, Moses is to the Israelites, and Muhammad is to Islam.

Legend has it that when Patrick was near death, St. Brigit came to him with a beautiful burial shroud that she herself had woven. It has often been written that they were very close and had deeply loved each other ever since Brigit came to hear Patrick preach when she was young. Supposedly his last benediction was for Brigit's nuns.

Christianity then took off in Ireland with fervent enthusiasm, for, as we've mentioned earlier, the new religion was quite similar to previous Celtic beliefs, and was embraced heartily by the Celtic peoples. The ascetic way of life was attractive to the Irish, and now with Patrick's work and encouragement, all elements were in place to produce a phenomenal monastic setting, a distinctly Irish form of Christianity that would bring to Europe a new awakening and era of learning.

Saint Enda of Inishmore and the Aran Islands, Saint Brigit of Kildare (just mentioned), Saint Brendan the Navigator, and Saint Columba (Colmcille) of Iona were all dedicated followers of Patrick. They and their followers founded extremely influential monasteries throughout Ireland and the European continent.

Saint Enda, Saint Finian, Saint Brigit, and Saint Kevin:

We've been discussing several of the early Irish Saints (sometimes they're referred to as the Celtic or Irish-Celtic Saints). The terminology of "Saint" was used in pre-medieval times to denote clerics of great piety or purity. No Roman Catholic Saints were canonized until centuries later, and none of these early Irish Saints were canonized by Rome, not even St. Patrick. A bit later we'll discuss some of the differences that developed between Roman Catholicism and the early Celtic Christian Church.

Eighth century historians divided the Irish Saints into three distinct groups, the first being St. Patrick and the other clerics of the early Christian tradition whom we've just discussed. The second group included the founders of the great monasteries and centers of learning and the third group encompassed the deeply ascetic hermit monks who left the great monasteries and went off alone in the original Egyptian or Judean tradition.

Much of Ireland was still pagan at the time of Patrick's death, and many of the Druids began reclaiming their powers. The immediate followers of Patrick were sincere, pious, and enthusiastic, but none of them had his great charisma or magnetism. The one to bridge the gap between the first and second groups, the one called the Father of Irish Monasticism, was St. Enda.

Enda studied at Candida Casa, St. Ninnian's School in Whithorn, which was located in present day Scotland. When he returned to Ireland, he asked his brother-in-law, King Aengus of Munster, for the Aran Islands, off the coast of County Galway, for the purpose of building his church. King Aengus said he would prefer to have Enda remain and preach at Cashel. The elderly Saint Ailbe then spoke up in Enda's behalf and made the ground rise up to show Aengus how fair and beautiful were the Aran Islands, as Aengus had never seen them and was afraid for Enda's safety. When King Aengus saw the beauty of the islands he immediately granted them to Enda.

Christianity had taken hold in Ireland with very little resistance and virtually no bloodshed—something that cannot be said for other regions. Because of this and the Irish Monks emphasis on scholarship and ascetic piety, Irish martyrdom is known as "White Martyrdom", as opposed to the "Red Martyrdom" associated with Rome, Jerusalem, and other areas of violent conversion.

Enda came to Inishmore, the largest of the Aran Islands around 480. The climate there is very mild as the islands are washed by the Gulf Stream. Flowers bloom year-around and occasionally you can even see rather scrawny palm trees growing there—from seeds possibly washed from Florida or the Caribbean. The climate is almost Mediterranean for three-quarters of the year, much milder than the Irish mainland.

The soil is manufactured from the rich limestone sand and seaweed and is extremely fertile, but heavily rock-laden. The Rock Walls and structures covering the islands pay tribute to virtually thousands of man-hours of laborious effort. The monastery built by Enda became renowned throughout the all of Europe and both ascetics and scholars began coming in great numbers. Eventually, half the island was devoted to the monastery of Enda and the other half was devoted to ten satellite or daughter monasteries, each with its own Bishop or superior, but all under the direct authority of Enda until his death in 530.

Enda was very strict and a great educator. The Monks' days were divided into set periods of prayer, labor, and sacred study. They cleared and planted these rock-laden fields entirely by hand. They ate together in silence and their diet consisted of oats and barley, along with the fish they caught. They ate no flesh and drank no wine.

The fame of St. Enda's Monastery spread over the entire Christian world and most of his students came from the European continent, whereto they would eventually return and spread the word of the Saints' sanctity and scholarship. It is said that over 120 Saints are buried in the cemetery on Inishmore. It is true that the Roman Legions never invaded Ireland, but several came to Enda's Monastery to study, and at least five are also buried in the cemetery there.

Among Enda's Irish disciples there were several that would carry on, and even surpass, the work that he had begun. Some of the most notable of these include Finian of Clonard, Ciaran of Clonmacnoise, Kevin of Glendalough, and the famed Brendan the Navigator, who came to Enda and prayed for the three days and three nights before beginning his voyage across the western seas to find the Land of Promise.

In 515, Finian established his monastery at Clonard on the banks of the Boyne River in County Meath. Finian was an excellent teacher and organizer. It is said he studied under David, Gildas, and Cadoc in Wales, as well as Enda. When he returned to Ireland he discovered that he was already known with followers awaiting his return, including the King of Leinster who had planted a great orchard of apples at the place Finian chose for the monastery. Nothing today remains of the Sixth Century Monastery, as unfortunately it was directly in the path of the Viking raids of the Ninth Century, The Anglo-Norman invasions of the Twelfth Century (led by Strongbow, the Earl of Pembroke and later by King Henry II himself), the agents of the dissolution of Henry VIII, and then of course there was Oliver Cromwell who pretty much destroyed whatever was left in the Boyne Valley. At one point however, there were over three thousand monks living at Clonard.

From these, it must be understood there were hundreds of disciples, including those termed the "Twelve Apostles of Ireland", which included the extremely influential Columba (or Colmcille), in addition to the others we've mentioned. Finian was an ascetic in the tradition of the Egyptian Fathers, believing in simplicity, prayer, sacred scholarship, fasting, and labor that insured the self-sufficiency of the monastery. A part of every monk's day was usually spent in the scriptorium, mostly copying the rare vellum manuscripts onto parchment made from goat, sheep, or other hides. These parchments, the quill pens used, the natural pigments, and the carbon ink were all made by the scribes themselves. This was the beginning of the production of the world's oldest and most beautifully illuminated manuscripts.

Finian's School was open to everyone who wished to learn. Study was in Latin by this time, and consisted mostly of Biblical interpretations, with some time given to the Greek and Roman Classics, Virgil, Homer, Aristotle, Plato, Horace, Cicero, etc.

The presence of women in the monasteries was not shunned in Ireland near as much as it was elsewhere. St. Patrick's entourage included several women and by the sixth century there were already a number of convents, the most famous of which was surely that of Ireland's female Patron Saint, Brigit of Kildare. She was born around 450 in County Louth, the daughter of a pagan chieftain, Dubhtach, and a female indentured servant. The King's wife was extremely jealous and made him sell the beautiful child. The sale of young Brigit was negotiated by a Druid, whom ultimately placed her into the home of one of his own Christian uncles.

All over Ireland Christian women were living with pagan relatives and Brigit decided to establish a monastery where these women could study and be at peace. She asked the King for the region known as the Curragh (today the center of Irish Horse Racing), County Kildare and built her monastery on the edge of this vast grassland. At first the king resisted but was then overcome by Brigit's incredible beauty as the story is told, and relented.

Brigit retained one very curious pagan rite, which is probably why today her legends are intermingled with the pagan goddess of the same name. She maintained a sacred fire out in front of her church. The flame burned day and night and was the responsibility always of twenty nuns. Supposedly the fire burned for seven hundred years until it was extinguished by the Anglo Norman Archbishop

Henry de Londres (Henry of London), in the year 1220. It was later rekindled and burned again until the dissolution of the monasteries by direction of England's King Henry VIII in 1540.

Brigit's monastery, church and convent became models for several early Irish monasteries and were visited by many monks seeking direction for establishment of their own monasteries including Finian and Brendan (whom we've briefly mentioned and will discuss in a bit more detail here in a moment). Brigit also traveled extensively founding numerous churches and convents, becoming a role model for thousands of Christian women.

One of those visiting Kildare was a shy gentle youth by the name of Kevin, whom Brigit took under her guidance, almost as a mother, giving him great counsel. He was born in 498, and lived to be 120 years of age, according to recorded accounts, however he may well have been a composite again of himself and one of his students assuming his name. By the age of twelve he displayed extreme piety, purity, and asceticism.

Wishing to retire from the world and lead a life of solitary contemplation, he ventured into the Wicklow Mountains. He there built a cell on bare rock, but it wasn't long before pilgrims sought him out, hearing of his great piety and purity. He then moved two more times before settling in the area called Glendalough (The Valley of Two Lakes), where he took up residence in a cave which was barely large enough for a man's body. This cave is known today as St. Kevin's Bed.

He prayed with all the animals of nature. Often birds perched on his head and shoulders as they did with St. Francis of Assisi, and it is said that one bird built a nest in his hand and he left it undisturbed until the young were born and flew away. Animals brought him food and protected him day and night.

St. Kevin's Church located at Glendalough (Valley of the Two Lakes) in County Wicklow. The original monastery here was founded in the Sixth Century by St. Kevin and is still to this day a destination for pilgrims from around the world. This is the only church in Ireland with the round tower incorporated into the church itself.

Kevin was of course found again as the stories of his great piety spread, and his monastic school that was established around these two lakes became a haven for students from everywhere in the western world, housing at one time over two thousand monks. Thousands of people yet today make annual pilgrimages to Glendalough, an extremely serene and spiritually peaceful valley. Little remains of Kevin's original monastery, but much was rebuilt from the time of his death up until the twelfth century, including an elaborately ornamented stone priory built in 1162 by St. Lawrence O'Toole (an Irish canonized Saint).

Another of St. Finian's Twelve Apostles was Ciaran, the founder of the Monastery at Clonmacnoise (meaning the fields of the hogs of Nos) on the River Shannon. He was born in 516 in County Roscommon and also studied under Enda at the Aran Islands, who was the one that directed him to build his church at Clonmacnoise. Ciaran lived only seven years after founding Clonmacnoise, dying in 549, at the age of thirty-three. Clonmacnoise however became, by the time of Charlemagne (c. 800 A.D.), one of the most illustrious schools of learning in the Christian world, a center of fabulous scholarship, art and literature.

At one point it was an elaborate monastic city with at least 105 buildings, many of which were destroyed by the Anglo-Normans in 1179. The city was burned at least thirteen times, pillaged by the Vikings eight times, attacked by the feuding Irish themselves at least twenty-seven times, and pillaged by the agents of the dissolution, sent by King Henry VIII in the 1540's, who carried away everything including the window glass. In spite of all this, the remains today are still quite extensive considering, and stand as an ancient silent shrine to long-ago grandeur.

Many of the grand Sixth and Seventh Century Monasteries saw their greatest growth following the deaths of their founders. Their work was carried forward by a number of serious and scholarly followers, including St. Brendan, St. Columba, and St. Columbanus.

A section of an eighth century church ruins and a round tower located at Glendalough.

Saint Brendan the Navigator:

For some reason the Irish Monks always seemed to possess something of a traveling spirit, believing they must always carry the faith forward. Beginning with St. Patrick, they nearly all were compelled to travel and seek out new converts and build churches and monasteries in regions previously without the Christian influence. Many had a difficult time staying in one location, always curious and always trying to expand the boundaries.

Brendan the Navigator was born into a sea-faring family living on a peninsula stretching out into Tralee Bay, County Kerry, and always had the sea in his heart. He was born in 484 to a pagan family, and was fostered out by the age of two to St. Ida, who it is said remained in a state of perpetual martyrdom by letting stag beetles continually feed upon her body.

At the age of seven Brendan began study under the tutelage of Bishop Erc in Galway, who ordained him a priest at age sixteen. The king of Ardfert then granted him a plot of land in County Kerry, only approximately five miles from his original home. There he founded a monastery with a small group of followers. It is also said that Bishop Erc instilled in him a tremendous fear of women, as all his life Brendan never associated with any women other than his sister, Brigit, in whose monastery and arms he would eventually pass. Nothing remains today of this original monastery.

Since a very young age, he often perceived the need to be closer to God, always loved the sea, and believed the best avenue to redemption was to lead the life of an exile. There had been tales well before the time of Brendan about the land called "Tir na n'Og"—The land of youth and promise. (Following the coming of Christianity it was believed to be God's Garden of Eden on Earth). There is also evidence that the Irish Monks never believed that the earth was flat, but always knew it was a continuum. (Just one example of the many fears and superstitions that plagued Europe and kept many people rather ignorant all through the Middle Ages and beyond).

One night Brendan had a vision that he climbed a high mountain (now called Brendan Mountain on the Dingle Peninsula) and saw far out to sea a noble island with angels continuously rising from it. He then summoned all the monks to the monastery related this vision, and began preparing to set sail with those monks wishing to join him. They smeared rosin and pitch all over their very light, ox-hide boats, both inside and outside. Each of the boats was equipped with three rows of oars and sails made from animal hides. Each boat carried twenty monks and enough food and water for forty days.

They first went to Inishmore where they prayed for three days and received the blessing of Enda, before setting sail westward into the unknown. The voyagers kept journals and notes that were then compiled into a Tenth Century work entitled "Navigatio de Sancti Brendani de Abati". It was a great literary success and was studied extensively by Christopher Columbus prior to his voyage. It is documented he even came to Ireland to visit two monasteries and study the monks' original notes before he set sail.

These notes spoke of things thought unimaginable by the people of the day, such as huge pillars of incredibly beautiful light (icebergs which were west of Greenland and over halfway across the Atlantic and had never been recorded previously); and, Flaming Islands arising out of the sea (this spoke of the ever-occurring formation of the volcanic islands off the coast of Iceland, at that time called Thule—which is still occurring today). Up until the Sixteenth Century this region was considered to be the gateway to Hell. Brendan's Monks also first spoke of many fish the size of islands (whales), which travel in great numbers just off the North American coast. These and other phenomena have since been written about, documented and substantiated many times, first by the Norsemen and the Danes in the Ninth and Tenth Centuries, who also made the crossing to North America and also stated that Brendan had done this earlier (they had learned of this and other navigations from the Monks following their invasions of Ireland); and, later from a variety of seafaring traders from northern Europe and the region of the Mediterranean who ventured westward in the early Middle Ages. It is believed by most scholars that Brendan and his followers could never have known of such phenomenon if they had not in fact made the voyage

It must also be noted here that the "Navagatio" was a compilation of more than just the Irish Monks' seafaring adventures. It contained some rather fanciful and dramatic representations as well, such as the "Island of Man-eating Mice". When it was taken from the Monks' notes and written the authors most likely embellished the stories somewhat to make the work more exciting, and perhaps more marketable.

Dunbrody Abbey is located in County Wexford and was built by Richard fitzGilbert de Clare (Strongbow) in the latter half of the Twelfth Century for his uncle, a Cistercian monk, who was the first Abbot here and was also buried here in 1205. Dunbrody Abbey is quite impressive and can be seen from well off in a distance.

Brendan's voyage was probably possible due to the types of boats they employed. They were very light and very tight and rode across the waves like big baskets, even in the heaviest seas. In the sixth century this voyage would not have been considered nearly as miraculous as it is today. Many had sailed the seas in search of exile (the Irish Monks knew of the voyages of the Greek explorer, Pytheas of Marsailles, who in 300 B.C.E., discovered the "farthest islands" a full six days sail west of Briton). You must also remember that among these people there was virtually no fear. They were secure in their faith and miracles were expected. After seven years Brendan returned to Ireland and established several Monasteries in the Provinces of Connacht and Munster. He is also referred to as Brendan of Clonfert, after his best-known monastery, which was located in southeast County Galway. Today there is a beautiful Twelfth-Century Stone church located there, highly ornamented in the Irish Romanesque style.

Brendan died in 577 at the age of ninety-three, at the convent of Annagh-down in County Galway that he had built for his sister, Brigit. He was one of the great saintly Christian heroes for many centuries—all through the Middle Ages—and is still to this day considered remarkable for his achievements by all the scholars studying him. He was both a respected religious leader and the romantic adventurer.

Saint Colmcille (Columba) of Iona:

Another Saint extremely influential in spreading the Irish Monastic tradition of faith and scholarship was Saint Columba. He was born in 521, the great-grand-son of Niall of the Nine Hostages, the king who first took Patrick captive. His baptismal name was Crimthann, which means wolf. Because of his great piety Crimthann was given the name Colmcille by many of his early friends, which when translated means "Dove of the Church" or "Dove of the Sanctuary"; and, throughout history he has become best known as Columba, which is the Latin version of Colmcille.

St. Columba first studied with Enda on the Aran Islands and then under Finian at Clonard where he became a priest and known as one of the twelve Irish apostles. He became a great leader and an exceptional organizer. Following his ordination he returned to Donegal. His cousin who was the king gave him a beautiful hillside on the banks of the River Foyle, where the king himself often held court. The place was called Doire-Calgaich (the Oak-woods of Calgach) and today this hillside forms the original city of Derry, County Derry. Columba built his first monastery there in 546, building the church high on a hill in a beautiful stand of oak trees. Columba, like most of the Irish Monks loved to commune with nature and shared a special tenderness with the other creatures of nature.

St. Columba was a renowned poet and authority on the history of Ireland. Irish monastic education was much more liberal and varied than that on the continent. The pagan classics were studied in Ireland, and a special reverence was paid to the bards and poets, perpetuating their works in their own native languages. The rest of Europe for the most part studied only in Latin and the old languages were forgotten, lost, or at least unrecognizably mutated. Columba studied under a master poet by the name of Gemman who trained him in the old Druidic style.

At one point he returned to visit Finian and was shown a copy of the psalms that had just arrived from Rome. It was believed to be the first copy of either the Vulgate (early Holy Bible written or compiled by St. Jerome) or the Psalter that was ever seen in Ireland. Finian treasured the great manuscript and allowed Columba to read it, but had forbidden him to copy it. Well, Columba stayed up all night a few nights and secretly copied it. When this was discovered, Finian demanded the copy as well as the original. Columba refused to surrender the copy and the matter was taken before Diarmait the High King at Tara. Diarmait ruled in Finian's favor, stating "to every cow belongs her calf, and to every book belongs its copy". Many believe this is the first recorded copyright ruling. A short time later during a game of hurling, a son of the King of Connacht accidentally killed one of Diarmait's sons. He ran to the sanctuary of Columba's church for protection, where Diarmait's soldiers defiled the church by breaking in and seizing the man. This infuriated Columba.

Columba encouraged an army to be organized and march against Diarmait. The two armies met at Culdreimhne in County Sligo and over three thousand men were killed. This ultimately led to the fall of Diarmait and that of Tara itself as a kingdom. The victorious army wished to place Columba on the throne as the High King of Ireland, but Columba refused the position, being extremely remorseful. His self-reproach was exceptionally severe and he concluded that his only restitution could be to convert as many souls as had perished due to his actions. He decided on self-imposed exile and chose the land of modern-day Scotland, which was called Alba or Pictland at that time. Scotland was during that period mainly ruled by the Picts (basically a combination of Celtic people and an earlier Neolithic race).

Columba left Ireland in 563, accompanied by twelve clerics. (This became traditional with the Irish monks, following in the pattern of Jesus Christ.) They first made landfall in Alba at a place called Kintyre, but soon decided to move on and landed at the island of Iona, about one mile off the large island of Mull, and approximately seventy-five miles from Ireland. The earth here is more fertile than one would suspect due to the high concentration of lime in the shell sand, and the waters are full of fish and seals, a plentiful supply of meat, hides, and burnable oil. St. Columba built his monastery on a high hill overlooking the eastern coast.

Columba's Rule was strict and he also placed a great emphasis on the work of the scribes in the scriptorium. It is said that at one point Columba had over two thousand Monks working in the scriptoriums. In 806, when the Norse raided Iona and killed eighty-six of the Monks, the survivors went back to Ireland and founded the Monastery at Kells County Meath that produced the great illuminated manuscript known as The Book of Kells (one of the oldest copies in existence of the four gospels—from the seventh or eighth century). Several researchers believe The Book of Kells was possibly started on Iona and then brought to Kells and completed following the Norse raids on Iona. The followers of Columba created some of the most beautiful illuminated manuscripts the world has ever known, including also the Book of Durrow and the Book of Armagh(all of these are currently housed in the library at Trinity College, Dublin).

Iona was situated directly on the edge of the lands controlled by the pagan picts, and Columba knew the monastery's survival depended on his gaining the favor of the pagan king, Brude (I'm sure following the style of Patrick). Columba went to Inverness, the Pict's capital, but Brude barred the gates on the advice of his Druid Broichan. According to legend, Columba made the sign of the cross and the gates flew open. Columba was then received with great respect by the king, and from that day forward Brude admired, honored and supported this holy man. They spoke often in an atmosphere of peace and a new awakening came to the land of the Picts. The Irish Monks brought great knowledge to the Picts in addition to the Christian faith, including advanced agricultural practices, knowledge of medicine and medicinal herbs, and their first educational system.

Cloister of Sligo Abbey, a Dominican Friary, located in Sligo town centre. It was built in 1252-1253 by Maurice Fitzgerald, as was the medieval town of Sligo, but Sligo had been a settlement dating to earliest pre neolithic times. The landscape is very beautiful here and is an ideal location, linking Lough Gill with the sea via the Garavogue River, and Connacht to Donegal by land.

Looking across from out on Coney Island at Ben Bulben and the village of Rosses Point, County Sligo.

Columba's monks traveled throughout Alba and the Highlands, preaching and teaching. One of his disciples, Cormac, sailed around the northern tip of Scotland, sailed across the extremely dangerous passage between the Atlantic and the North Sea, and settled on Orkney Island where he established a monastery and preached to the Picts. He also sailed as far as the Faeroe Islands, Iceland and Greenland. Cormac eventually ended up back at Iona, but Columba told him his work was in Durrow and sent him there.

Columba was primarily responsible for the Christianization of Scotland and in 574, Aidan, the grandson of Fergus, became the first Christian King of Scotland. He and Columba formed an alliance, which was cultural and political, as well as religious. This ultimately led to an alliance between Christian Ireland and Christian Scotland that would endure for centuries, sharing Saints and Scholarship; and, uniting against the invasions of the Saxons, Vikings and Danes.

In 597, thirty-four years after Columba came to Iona, Rome and Pope Gregory I sent the papal emissary Augustine to convert the Saxons and Britons. He became the first Bishop of Canterbury, but was not well received by any but the Saxons. In approximately 604, a follower of Columba, Aidan of Iona, was instructed by King Oswald of Northumbria, to establish a monastery at Lindisfarne (eastern Scotland/Britain), which for the next thirty years became the stronghold of Christian scholarship in northern Briton. It was inevitable that the two great Christian traditions, that of Rome and that of the Irish or Celts, were about to clash.

The Irish church had never been directly under the control, nor particularly obedient, to Rome. The Irish ways were considered suspect by Rome, who was basically power-orientated, creating also a great political and economic machine. The Irish asceticism, love of nature, and emphasis on truth did not necessarily fit into this machine. The Romans had created a new calendar and recalculated the date of Easter to fit into this calendar. This Irish still celebrated Easter according to the original calculations. There were also a number of liturgical and organizational questions on which the two churches differed, as well as the tonsure (the way the Monks shaved their heads).

Tensions mounted and in 664, the King of Northumbria, Oswy, called a synod at the monastery founded by Hilda at Whitby, to settle the arguments. At the Synod of Whitby, Bishop Colman, Abbot of Lindisfarne, presented the Irish position, with the English and/or Roman position being delivered by Wilfred, the Abbot of Ripon Monastery. Wilfred was shrewd, prepared for argument, and claimed the whole world outside of these islands was on the side of Rome. Colman had not really planned nor prepared, relying on his eloquence and the absolute correctness or truth of his position. The deciding blow was struck when Wilfred quoted Jesus as saying, "Thou art Peter, and upon this rock I will build my church, and the gates of hell shall not prevail against it, and to thee I will give the keys of my kingdom in heaven." (Rome of course had always claimed that Peter founded the church there, was the first Bishop of Rome, and is even buried beneath St. Peter's Basilica). Basically, King Oswy was afraid to rule against this argument and ruled in favor of Wilfred. This was a major decision basically affecting Christian worship for all time. Many theologians believe Celtic Christianity may well have been the purest form of organized Christianity yet known.

In defeat, Bishop Colman took the Irish monks from Lindisfarne, went to Iona, and then on to Galway where he founded a monastery on the island of Inishbofin. Lindisfarne has the dubious distinction of then becoming the first monastery raided and destroyed by the Vikings in 793. It was however, revived by the Normans in the eleventh century and is today something of a Riviera-like tourist attraction.

As you can see, a great deal of historical influence can be attributed to Saint Columba. He died in 597, after a series of Norse raids beginning in 595.

His remains were taken to Dunkeld in the Scottish Highlands, and then eventually removed to Downpatrick, where they are entombed with those of St. Patrick and St. Brigit. In literature one will see Colmcille spelled several different ways—Colm Cille, Cholm Cille, Columcille.

The quite elaborate and well preserved Kells Monastery in County Kilkenny.

Saint Columbanus of Luxeuil:

I'd like to briefly discuss one more of the great traveling Irish Saints. He is St. Columbanus of Luxeuil, the founder of monasteries from Briton, through Gaul, and into Italy, Germany and Switzerland. He was born in 543, in Leinster. His mother had a vision before he was born in which she saw the sun rising from her bosom to light up the world. She took exceptional care of Columbanus who came to be known as the "Child of Light". Often in his life he would seek out desolate places where he could pray and commune with the forests and the wild animals of nature.

He first studied at a monastery located at Lough Erne in County Fermanagh, where the Abbot was Sinell, a disciple of Finian's. There he learned the Scriptures well and wrote sacred poetry. Sinell then recommended him for Comgall's excellent school located at Bangor, where many of the finest minds of the age were then gathered. He must have liked the atmosphere because he stayed there approximately thirty years, attaining the position of Principal Teacher. He was much loved by everyone and valued most highly by Comgall.

At forty-eight years of age the urge again came to him to seek contemplative exile. He had learned a great deal, both scholastically or academically, and regarding the workings of a monastery. In 591 he landed on the coast of Briton, and made his way south into Burgundy—at that time within the kingdom of the Merovingians and inhabited by the Franks. The King of the Franks at that time was Childebert II, great-grandson of Clovis I, founder of the Merovingian dynasty, but the real power was held by Childebert's mother Queen Brunhilda.

The king asked Columbanus to preach a sermon in Latin and was so moved by it that he asked the monk to stay there. He was given land in a region which is today located on the border between Switzerland and Germany. It was the location of an old Roman fort called Anegrates (today Annegray) and the monks rebuilt the walls of the old fort, as well as what had been a temple to the goddess Diana, which was rededicated to the patron saint of the region St. Martin of Tours. The life there was extremely tough. Europe, and especially this region, was very combative—far more so than Ireland. There were constantly raids perpetuated by the violent warlords.

The Monks had nothing worth taking except food and the Monks were often on the verge of starvation. They were very near death at one point when all of a sudden a man showed up with two large horses laden with food. Quite some time earlier this man's wife had been near death and the Monks prayed for her and she recovered. The man wanted to show his appreciation. After this event many of the region's inhabitants began bringing their illnesses to the monastery and soon hundreds were flocking to the monastery to be healed. They were fascinated by the mysticism of the spiritual message and the peaceful, passive nature of the Monks, both concepts quite foreign to a people with only an aggressive, pagan, and violent history.

Columbanus has always been revered throughout this region. In 1945, the sculptor Claude Granges erected a large bronze of Columbanus that stands outside the current Thirteenth Century Church in the city of Luxeuil, which is today still a major health resort and center of healing.

We all know how politics seems to have destroyed many good things over the centuries, well this also happened at Luxeuil. Warring for lands and kingdoms was the way of life in this region and two of Brunhilda's sons wanted these particular lands. Brunhilda wanted Columbanus to baptize two illegitimate heirs and when Columbanus refused, the Monks were expelled from Luxeuil and Annegray in 610.

They were going to make their way back to Ireland, but literally missed the boat, and wandered back across France (or Gaul), and eventually ended up on a boat heading up the Rhine River to Lake Constance. They arrived there in 612. In 613, Columbanus and his Monks headed out across the Alps, an incredibly cold and dangerous journey, but they eventually reached the Plain of Lombardy, ruled by Duke Agilulf, who held court and resided in Milan. He liked the courageous Monks and asked them to stay.

Columbanus founded his final monastery at a place called Bobbio, where the River Bobbio met another mountain stream and formed a beautiful valley. After the death of Brunhilda, the Frankish King Lothar II asked Columbanus to return to Luxeuil, but he refused, as he had become heavily involved in the Arian Heresy in Italy. In 615, he retired to a cave alone high in the mountains where he died in the company of the animals he loved. He is buried in a beautiful marble tomb located at the picturesque stone church in Bobbio. Columbanus had brought great faith and scholarship throughout a vast region of violent and pagan warlords.

Saints like Columba and Columbanus were men of profound faith and spirituality, but they were also exceptional scholars and organizers. Each monastery was a self-sufficient entity ruled by an Abbot—something of a small town if you will; and, in Ireland as was mentioned earlier these were basically the only towns and most definitely the largest settlements. Hence, they became the first targets of the Norse raids and invasions, which began in the late Eighth Century.

The Viking and Norman Invasions

The Norse and the Danes:

The period of the Vikings, which began in the Eighth Century, lasted almost four hundred years. The first Vikings to come to Ireland were the Norsemen from the regions of Norway and Sweden. Their homelands were becoming over-populated, the lands were not particularly fertile, and economic crisis was setting in. They set out looking for more fertile lands in a more favorable climate. They were basically an adventurous, warring, and pagan people.

They had first gone to Iceland where they encountered the settlements of the Irish Monks and learned of the warm fertile lands located just a bit further south. The first Irish contact with the Norsemen came in 794 or 795, there are varying accounts, when they attacked and devastated the Island of Rechru (currently Lambay) just offshore from present day Howth head, slightly north of Dublin. They sacked the monastery there that had been one of the first founded by St. Columba. Ironically in the same year, these raiders from Scandanavia also plundered Iona, the most famous, scholarly, and elaborate of the monasteries founded by St. Columba. These Vikings then went back to their homeland carrying tales of wealth and land.

In 823, several groups returned. One party raided the monastery at Skellig Michel, off the coast of County Kerry, killing all the monks living there. Others raided the coasts of Wales, Cornwall, and Gaul, especially the area later to become known as Normandy (French for lands of the Norse). Their longboats were very fast and didn't draw much water. Therefore they could sail right up onto the beaches, and also up the many rivers and streams.

Around 835 they sailed up the River Liffey and eventually came to the place where the Liffey meets a smaller stream, the River Poddle. There was a Celtic village located there and the Norsemen were impressed with its location and the fertility of the soil. The Vikings were not only interested in plunder and booty, they were also interested in trade, and the establishment of homes and trading centers. In 837, they constructed an earthen fort there on the highest hill (which is now the location of Dublin Castle and a portion of the Viking settlement is still located under the castle). They named the area Dubh linn, meaning "Black Pool", after the dark color of the water found in the bog. The Norsemen minted silver coins here, the first ever produced in Ireland. For the next two hundred years Dublin would remain a city of Norsemen and Danes. Remember, the Irish Capital at that time was Armagh. Dublin also in fact ultimately became a successful Danish trading center with quite extensive movement for many years between Dublin, the Isle of Man, and York in northern Britain, which was the Danes capital in Northumbria.

Originally sixty ships had sailed up the Liffey and another sixty had sailed up the River Boyne, all under the command of Tuirgeis (also called Thorgest in historical literature), who was one of the most famous and capable leaders in Nordic history. Tuirgeis next headed for the Irish capital of Armagh where he drove out the followers of St. Patrick around the year 845. He converted the church into a pagan temple and declared himself the High Priest. He next set off for Clonmacnoise, Ireland's second most holy city, and did the same thing there. He placed his wife Otta on the throne at Clonmacnoise and she supposedly declared herself High Priestess and daily screamed scathing oracles and magical incantations, insulting and condemning the Irish.

Shortly after this, still in 845, Tuirgeis was taken prisoner by Malachy (or Maelsechlainn in Irish), King of Meath, and drowned in Loch Owel, supposedly an act of the Irish Saints. The remaining Norsemen had to fight all the way up the River Shannon and across to the Sligo coast where their ships were waiting. Tuirgeis' followers were almost exclusively of Norwegian background.

Meanwhile the Danes, who were more organized than the Norse, were plundering England and had, as mentioned, established their capital in Northumbria—at York. In 847, the Danes invaded the east coast of Ireland with about fifty ships. At first the Irish called all these invaders "Genti", meaning Heathen, or "Lochlannaigh" (meaning "Men of the Lakes"—as does the word "Viking"). But they soon began distinguishing between the Lochlannaigh and the "Danair". The Norwegians, or Lochlannaigh, were also called the White Heathens, and the

Danes, or Danair, were also called the "Black Heathens", primarily because of the color of their hair.

In 850, the Danes seized and plundered Dublin. In 852, the Norwegians regained control, under their mighty warlord known as "Amahlaobh" in Irish, or "Olaf the White" throughout most other historical accounts. The Norwegians then established several other settlements along the east coast, including Strangford and Carlingford in the north of Ireland, and Waterford, Wicklow, Cork, and Wexford in the south. Gradually, these coastal cities became more important and influential than the interior cities, such as Tara and Armagh. In the second half of the Ninth Century, the Danes sailed up the River Shannon and founded the city of Limerick, which flourished and came to exert great influence throughout that region.

Both of these peoples were slowly adopting Christianity as they avidly intermarried with the native Irish (many of the Norse took Christianity back to Scandanavia with them, and a grandson of "Olaf the White", Olaf II, became "Saint Olaf", the Patron Saint of Norway, canonized in 1164). The Norsemen assimilated the Irish ways more readily and quickly than the Danes, and eventually even became allies with the Irish against the Danes.

During the first part of the Tenth Century, the Danes came to control large portions of the interior of Ireland. In 914, Danish reinforcements arrived at Waterford and they sailed up the Shannon River again all the way to Lough Ree, plundering and burning everything not Danish, including Clonmacnoise. Their leader was Tomrair, the son of the King of Denmark. Most history texts claim that Tomrair died a horrible tragic death, duly deserved.

King Cellachan of Cashel, whose reign as King of Munster began in 934, won back from the Danish invaders most of the Munster lands over the next decade. Cellachan was captured in 949, and rescued during the famous sea battle in the Bay of Dundalk in 950-951. The Danish Leader, Sitric, was drowned in this battle. Cellachan then proceeded directly to Dublin, overthrew the Danes there and, according to historical accounts took great quantities of Danish booty.

The most famous figure of the Danish Period, and one of the most famous in Irish History, was of course Brian Boru. He was born Brian mac Cenneidigh (son of Kennedy) in 941. He took the name of Boru from a town of which he was very fond located on the banks of the River Shannon. He was the youngest of twelve brothers. Ten of these brothers would be killed in battle. One of his brothers, Mahon, seized the throne of Cashel in 964. In 976, Brian at age thirty-five would become King of Munster and in three years would become the king of all of southern Ireland.

In 999, Brian united with Malachy II, his former rival, to defeat the Danes near Dunlavin in County Wicklow. Historical accounts claim that over seven thousand Danes were killed there. Brian and Malachy then captured, plundered and again burned Dublin. Malachy and Brian then again quarreled and in 1002, after Malachy discovered defections in his military ranks and conceded, Brian became the High King of all of Ireland. The Ui Neill dynasty also yielded the high kingship to him without a fight.

After driving the Danes from Ulster and reclaiming Armagh in 1004, the scribe, Maelsuthain, wrote in the Book of Armagh that Brian Boru was "Emperor of the Irish". Brian was an exceptional warrior and strategist, he built roads and churches, built schools and encouraged learning, and even sent emissaries all over the world to buy books.

Brian made a pact with the Dublin Danes and in exchange for their loyalty they were given land. Brian gave his daughter in marriage to Sigtryggr, his former opponent and leader of the Dublin Danes, and Brian himself married Sigtryggr's mother, Gormlaith, who according to history was exceptionally beautiful and seduced many men, being married five or six times—rather in the Cleopatra tradition (Brian was either her second or third husband). After Brian eventually got rid of her, she developed a deep hatred and according to some accounts was the eventual cause of Brian's death.

In 1014, Brian was seventy-three years old and facing the final great battle against the remaining foreign adversaries, who had gathered on the east coast near Clontarf with reinforcements from Normandy, Flanders, England, Cornwall, the Orkneys, the Shetlands, and the Hebrides. Brian wanted to lead the fight, but was persuaded by his son and his generals to remain behind the lines in a tent, under heavy guard.

Both armies were estimated to be approximately 20,000 men, but the Danish troops were much better armed and equipped. The Danes were winning at first, but then Malachy showed up with reinforcements and the tide was turned in favor of the Irish. As the Dane's were fleeing, Brian's guards were overrun and Brian was killed. Brian's whereabouts supposedly had been disclosed by Gormlaith. Brian supposedly killed his assassin, Brodar, before he died.

The next year, 1015, Malachy defeated the last of the hostile foreigners near Dublin and reigned in peace as High King of Ireland, until his death in 1022. All the Danes and Vikings that remained in Ireland then became peaceful, settled down, intermarried, and history says they became "more Irish than the Irish". They severed their ties with Scandanavia, gave up their pagan beliefs, and came to be known in Ireland as "Ostman" (men of the east). This is something that would soon anger the Norsemen's relatives, the Normans, who had much more easily gained control of southern England and the coast of France.

The Irish gave the Norsemen Christianity, civility, culture and language. The Norsemen taught the Irish their advanced shipbuilding skills (In Irish, virtually every word regarding shipbuilding or the parts of ships was originally a Norse word). The great shipyards of Donegal (In Irish "Dun na nGall", or "Fort of Foreigners") were established by these Norsemen; and, if there is yet today any predominantly Viking-influenced area in Ireland, it would be Donegal. The language dialect there is distinctly different and heavily Norse influenced.

All was rather peaceful for the next hundred-and-fifty years or so, until Henry II, the Norman King of England decided the Irish may revert back to their pagan ways and asked the English Pope, Nicholas Breakspeare, whom was now known as Adrian IV, permission to invade the island for the purpose of saving these poor wretched Irish souls.

Adrian IV, who was born in 1100 and reigned as Pope from 1154-1159, was the only Englishman to ever become Pope and he quickly issued the Papal Bull "Laudabiliter" authorizing Henry II to conquer the island of Ireland for the purpose of relieving the deplorable religious conditions and lack of morals.

The Norman English:

The Normans were basically Vikings or Norsemen who had conquered the coastal region of Gaul, or modern-day France, and had been living there for a couple hundred years. They so dominated the region that in 911, King Charles III of France ceded the land to them, and the Norse king, Rollo, became the first

Duke of Normandy. In exchange they agreed to give up piracy, adopt Christianity, as well as the customs and language of the French. Norman is the French equivalent of Norseman, and the region came to be called Normandie (lands of the Norse).

In 1066, the Anglo-Saxon king of England, Edward (The Confessor), died without an heir. His mother was a Norman. Edward's final words indicated that he wanted William, the Duke of Normandy, to succeed him. William was the illegitimate son of the former Duke of Normandy Robert I and a peasant girl. He was known throughout most of history as "William the Bastard" (but I suppose this became politically incorrect so it was changed to "William the Conqueror"). Anyway, the Anglo-Saxon assembly of England ignored King Edward's decree and named Harold Godwinsson the new king. This brought an immediate reaction from the very powerful Normans, especially after Godwinsson's army turned back a Viking invasion at Stamford Bridge, and on 14 October 1066, the forces of William defeated those of Godwinsson at the Battle of Hastings, and England became Norman with William being crowned King of England at Westminster Abbey on Christmas Day 1066. Henry II was the great-grandson of William (and the first of the Plantagenet dynasty which would rule England until the death of Richard III in 1485).

Henry II was actually asked by one of the Irish kings, Diarmuid MacMurrough, to invade Ireland and restore him as King of Leinster. He had been ousted because he had abducted another king's wife, by the name of Dervorgilla, in 1152. Several historical accounts stated she went along quite willingly, but whatever the case, much of history also says he stole her and was chastised. Henry was at the time fighting in French Aquitaine and couldn't be bothered, but gave Diarmuid a letter stating that any of the Norman warlords were welcome to help Diarmuid (Dermot) if they so desired.

Richard de Clare was the Norman/Welsh "Earl of Pembroke" and he was going broke. He was also known as "Strongbow", and he agreed to help MacMurrough in exchange for land, and MacMurrough's beautiful daughter's hand in marriage. Strongbow first sent to Ireland his two half-brothers, Robert Fitz Stephen and Maurice Fitz Gerald in the spring of 1169, with about four hundred archers and knights (Strongbow followed within the year). They were joined by Diarmuid MacMurrough's army of about five hundred and captured the Danish city of Wexford (on the third try).

Foreign mercenaries had always been brought into Ireland; and, as long as it didn't directly affect the other kings, these kings really didn't pay much attention.

Diarmuid's army then attacked another Danish city-Dublin. This got a little more attention, and King Roderick O'Connor then gathered an army. O'Connor was joined by about four hundred Waterford men, and they attacked the Norman forces. They were badly routed due to the Normans' superior weaponry and armor. The Normans took over forty prisoners, broke their arms and legs, and hurled them over the cliffs and into the sea. This got even more attention and a short time later Strongbow showed up with about twelve hundred more men.

The Normans then attacked Waterford, slaughtering most of the inhabitants. Strongbow married Diarmuid's daughter on the battlefield, standing in blood to glorify his victory, according to historic accounts. He then declared himself the King of Leinster, somewhat settled down and became quite comfortable. He liked Ireland and would not return to Normandy when summoned by King Henry II.

We mentioned earlier about Henry being upset by the fact that the previous Norsemen had settled out in Ireland becoming quite content, and according to history became "more Irish than the Irish". He was worried that the same thing might possibly be happening to Strongbow and his followers. This, along with the fact he had heard about Ireland's great beauty and fertility, made Henry decide to visit there himself. He took four hundred ships and nearly five thousand knights and soldiers, and landed at Waterford in October 1171. Most of the Irish chiefs were then forced to submit to Henry's authority, as they could provide no match for the Normans' superior military machine.

Henry then marched to Dublin and there set up his court, built a palace, and partied all winter long. He was a strong and brutal enforcer. In March 1172, he called a synod at Cashel where the Irish Bishops were forced to acknowledge Henry as "Lord Supreme" in Ireland. At Easter, Henry returned to England, leaving Strongbow in charge of Leinster, and others in charge elsewhere.

The Irish soon realized they had to do something, and began a campaign of subversion and gorilla warfare-type tactics. The Normans were brutal, burning the monasteries, killing entire villages, and building castles to protect themselves. Most of the castles still seen in Ireland yet today were built during this period.

In 1185, King Henry II appointed nineteen-year-old Prince John as "Lord of Ireland". He was young, abrasive, insulting, and obnoxious. He was permitted to stay for only a short period; and, in that time he seriously damaged the English cause and greatly strengthened and united the Irish cause.

The English royal house has quite often been rather turbulent over the years, to put it mildly. Henry II died in 1189, cursing his entire family. He had held his wife, Eleanor of Aquitaine, a prisoner for over ten years because he believed that she had plotted with three of his five sons to overthrow him; and, he hated his sons, two of whom would become future Kings of England, Richard ("The Lion-heart"), who upon the death of Henry became King of England in 1189, and John, who became king in 1199 while Richard was away on The Third Crusade and languishing in a Germanic prison after being taken captive by the Holy Roman Emperor, Henry VI. John took the throne in 1199, the same year that Donal MacCarthy of Desmond defeated the English of Munster and drove them from Limerick and the surrounding areas.

King John's Viceroy of Ireland, and Archbishop of Dublin, was a fellow named Henry of London. His only two passions were hunting deer and collecting money. He fleeced money from the English and the Irish alike. In order to build Dublin Castle, he closed several churches and confiscated their property, including the great center of learning, Glendalough, which was revered throughout Europe for its sanctity, scholarship, and as a major center for the study of both Greek and Latin. Henry of London became nicknamed "The Scorch Villain".

The Irish would still be deterred from neither their religious beliefs nor their culture, and more and more of the Normans were realizing the Irish ways were more peaceful and truthful than those of the Normans. They noted that while the Brehon Laws were used in Ireland, there was never one instance of a Brehon (judge) being corrupt, or taking a bribe, or favoring his friends and family. All decisions were based on honor, truth, and honesty; and, all the Irish happily accepted whatever ruling came down from the Brehons. This amazed the Normans, whose courts were based almost exclusively on favoritism and bribery.

More and more Normans intermarried with the Irish, adopted Irish dress, language and customs; and, fostered their children to Irish families and Scholars.

This worried and infuriated the proud and arrogant Normans and led to the institution of the Penal Laws, among the first and most famous of which were the "Statutes of Kilkenny" drafted in 1366-1367. These forbade Norman-Irish inter-marriages, the wearing of Irish clothing, the speaking of the Irish language, the display of any Irish customs such as music and dance, and even included a law passed by Parliament that forbade moustaches. The Irish and the rest of Europe found moustaches fashionable at this time, but the Normans all had clean-shaven upper lips and tried to demand the Irish do the same. The formal penalties for violation of the Penal Laws included death, quartering and disembowelment. These Normans, however, never realized the strength and determination of the Irish, as virtually none of the invaders of Ireland have up until this very day, and the Irish never attempted to comply with these laws. This harsh treatment only furthered the Irish cause, determination, resolve, and resilience.

Medieval Ireland to the Seventeenth Century

With all the attempted restrictions, and the oppression, intended by the Penal Laws, the actual lifestyles and activities of the Irish kings and their followers were disrupted and changed very little in the beginning. The Irish chieftain was in reality still a semi-nomadic person, spending a great deal of time out-of-doors, herding cattle and moving to better pastures, hunting, planting and tending food crops, or engaging in feasts and celebrations. The native Irish were very close to nature and readily felt more comfortable out in the open. The Irish chieftains habitually dined out-of-doors, in the tradition of the ancient Celtic warriors (or fianna), and continued to do so well into Elizabethan times, much to the horror of the more "refined" English populace. The English also thought that the diet of the Irish was barbaric and scandalous as they ate under-cooked meat, raw salads and greens, milk, cheese, and other dairy products (Irish butter has always been considered among the best in the world), while eating very little refined breads and pastries.

In the face of Norman advances, if an Irish noble or chieftain were forced to flee to the woods, their material situation would in fact change very little. This allowed for great resilience, an important quality that would serve the Irish well throughout their history. All noble Irish families also maintained the services of a poet or bard, whose task it was to orally recount, hence record and preserve, the legends and folktales; as well as keeping the positive aspects of Irish recovery forever present in the hearts and minds of the people. When these stories were later recorded, or written, they became the basis of a very mystical and dynamic literary tradition that has continued unbroken to this day.

As was previously mentioned, the Royal Family of England was at this time having an abundance of problems on virtually every front. Their problems certainly didn't die with Henry II. When his son John became king in 1199, the monarchy was faced with revolt from the people due to the extremely heavy tax burden the people had been forced to bear in order to support the ridiculous Crusades; and, even worse to ransom Richard from his captor, the Holy Roman Emperor Henry VI. In 1209 the Pope, Innocent III, excommunicated King John, and forced him to make several humiliating concessions to regain favor, including reducing England to the status of a Vatican fiefdom. The people of England didn't care for this at all, but the final straw was when the French defeated the English at the Battle of Bouvines in 1214.

John was overthrown and forced to sign the Magna Carta (Latin for "Great Charter") on 15 June 1215, which dramatically reduced the powers of the monarchy, granted a great many human rights, and reduced the excessive feudal dues. It also insured many privileges for the church. It specifically defined the Barons and landowners' obligations to the monarch and restructured the methods employed to administer justice. It was changed and reissued in 1216, 1217, and 1225. The Magna Carta was once annulled by the Pope, Honorius III (who took legal guardianship of King John's Infant son upon the death of John in 1216, and also persuaded King Philip II of France, John's intimate friend, not to invade England and place his own son on the throne). By the time the Welsh Tudors came to power in the fifteenth century (Owen Tudor c. 1400-1461 to Elizabeth I in 1603), it was nearly forgotten, but was rediscovered and reinterpreted by the Parliamentary Party in the seventeenth century as a significant democratic document. (Four original copies exist—two in the British Library, one in Salisbury Cathedral, and one in Lincoln Cathedral.) Anyway, history often has proposed that in 1215, most of the English people wanted to completely dissolve the monarchy, but it survived by a thread, with this being an extremely important point regarding future events in Ireland, America, Scotland, India, Africa, and elsewhere.

A rebellious and dissident Irish population always seeking liberty and freedom from oppression also posed a direct threat to the English crown, and in 1263, the crown of Ireland was offered to Haakon IV of Norway, a strong English ally. He was considered one of the most progressive and respected leaders in Europe at the time, as Norway was flourishing militarily, economically, politically, and culturally. He had taken control of the Faroe Islands, Iceland, and Greenland, but he died before being able to accept the crown of Ireland.

A counter to the great Norman fighting machine had been forming in the highlands of northern Scotland. They were families of professional mercenary soldiers, of a Norse/Gaelic/Pictish derivative, known as "galloglasses" ("galloglaigh" in Irish, meaning "foreign youth", later to become synonymous with "foreign troops"). They were highly trained and specialized, heavily armed, and the Irish chieftains began importing them for protection.

Needless to say the English were not free to vigorously enforce the Irish Penal Laws with much enthusiasm. The Irish for the most part ignored them, meeting at times with just enough brutality to reinforce the Irish resolve. For example, there were laws passed forbidding the Irish from engaging in any professional occupation, trade, commerce, or becoming a member of any of the guilds, but by the Fifteenth Century the native Irish made up the majority in the Craft and Merchant Guilds in Ireland. However, the bulk of the very important international markets and commerce were still controlled by the English. There were pockets of Irish Merchants in Italy, Spain, and especially France, but these accounted for a rather small percentage overall. However, they would play a quite prominent role in future events.

In 1348 and 1349, the Black Death decimated Ireland, as it did much of England and the continent, and by the beginning of the Fifteenth Century, the English sphere of authority and influence in Ireland was limited to a small strip of land approximately thirty miles long and twenty miles deep along the coast surrounding Dublin, known as "The Pale", and a few walled cities in the north, Enniskillen, Beal Feirste (Belfast), etc.

The tales of the voyages of St. Brendan were especially popular during this period, and inspired Christopher Columbus and others to set sail looking for new and wonderful lands. North America, Central America, and the West Indies were even called "Great Ireland" or "Greater Ireland" during this period in much of the literature. I believe it was previously mentioned that Christopher Columbus even visited Ireland and studied closely the notes of St. Brendan before beginning his voyage. He also took a number of Irish sailors along with him (Patrick Maguire was, as the story goes, an Irishman accompanying Christopher Columbus, who was supposedly the first to set foot on the new world).

Through this period the Irish also maintained their thirst for scholarship. The University of Paris was the major worldwide university at this time, closely followed by the University of Bologna, and both of these had a large concentration of Irish students, especially the University of Paris. Irish students and scholars were considered to be among the best in Europe regarding the subjects of astronomy, geography, mathematics, and medicine. Remember, nearly every Irish Gaelic chieftain employed an astronomer, geographer, and physician, as well as the poet or bard mentioned earlier. It is interesting to note that Duke Lionel, brother of the King of England, and sponsor of the Kilkenny Statutes, which had basically banned or forbidden virtually everything "Irish", employed a contingent of only Irish physicians and would let no other touch him. All during the Middle Ages, Ireland was known as the land of Saints and Scholars.

Still at this time, the Norman-English were intermarrying with the Irish and ever more adopting many of the Irish ways. The Norman family of the Geraldines, who became the extremely Irish "Fitzgeralds", played a major role in the history of Ireland. The Geraldines of Kildare held lands all the way from County Down in the north, to at least County Carlow in the south, and west to Limerick. They ruled the area of Desmond in south Munster as a totally independent Monarchy. They even maintained their own Navy with dozens of ships.

The Geraldines were also considered Great Scholars and intermingled with the Irish Scholars enthusiastically, again intermarrying and adopting the Irish lifestyle as we've mentioned. They promoted all academic endeavors and even tried to establish another National University in the tradition of the University of Armagh, following its destruction (It had been the greatest center of European learning until the beginning of the Thirteenth Century, employing as many as 5,000 scholars from everywhere in the known world). Gerald, the Earl of Kildare's, new university was called "The College of the Blessed Virgin Mary at Maynooth". This Geraldine assimilation of the Irish ways again brought avid displeasure to the English.

Gerald Fitzgerald, the Eighth Earl of Kildare, who reigned from 1477 until 1513, was called "Gerald the Great" by the Irish. He was also known as Garait More, and was viewed at the time, as well as throughout most of history, as the unofficial king of Ireland during this period. There were at this time three main Anglo-Irish families controlling most of the land in Ireland outside of what is now Ulster (Ulster was controlled by the O'Neills), the Geraldines or Fitzgeralds of Leinster (earls of Kildare), the Fitzgeralds of Munster (earls of Desmond), and the Butlers (earls of Ormond). The Fitzgeralds supported the House of York (white roses) during the English "Wars of the Roses", and the Butlers supported the House of Lancaster (red roses). Gerald Fitzgerald thwarted King Edward IV's attempts to name an English Deputy to Ireland, and eventually had himself named Deputy. He formed many political alliances with the Gaelic chieftains, mostly through marriage arrangements. These greatly enhanced his influence. He eventually encouraged an invasion attempt of England after Henry VII, a Lancaster, became king that failed terribly. He was charged with treason and held in the Tower of London, but eventually was pardoned and reinstated as the Earl of Kildare. In 1492, Henry VII sent a new English Deputy to Ireland, Edward Poynings, and he would change everything dramatically for many years.

The Ninth Earl of Kildare, Gerait Og (also known as "Gerald the Younger"), was educated in England, appointed "Lord Deputy" of Ireland by his cousin Henry VIII in 1513 upon the death of Gerait's father, and would in the end become even more passionately Irish than his father had been. He was removed by Henry after seven years and charged by the English with sedition (inciting a rebellion against the state) and conspiracy.

From history we learn that Henry VIII had a very rough time from his earliest days. His father, Henry VII, was a rather demanding old fellow who had betrothed Henry to Catherine of Aragon, the daughter of King Ferdinand and Queen Isabella of Spain, only a few days before Henry VIII received the crown as King of England. Catherine had been the wife of Henry VIII's brother, Arthur, who had met an untimely death somehow. Henry's father wanted to keep the political alliance in tact between Spain and England hence Henry's marriage to Catherine was arranged. Catherine had several miscarriages and stillbirths and by 1527, their union had not produced any male heirs; and, only one female, Mary. Henry knew that the marriage of a man to his brother's wife was prohibited by biblical, canon and secular law (his marriage had required a special dispensation from Pope Julius II); and, he was convinced that God had cursed this union with Catherine. By 1527, he had decided to rid himself of Catherine and marry one of her ladies in waiting, Anne Boleyn. He wanted the Pope to grant an annulment but this was virtually impossible because Pope Clement VII was at that time being held prisoner by Charles V of the Holy Roman Empire; and, Charles V just happened to be Catherine's nephew. Henry was very confused, stressed out, and frustrated and he took out much of this frustration eventually on the Irish and all other Catholics. He renounced Catholicism and formed the Anglican Church of England.

Anyway, Gerait Og, the Earl of Kildare, was reappointed by Henry to the position of Lord Deputy of Ireland in 1525, to the people's delight; but, it was soon discovered that he had formed a secret alliance with Francis I, King of France, in 1523, to overthrow the English and drive them from Ireland and Scotland. The insurrection was delayed however when the Scottish troops under the Duke of Albany failed to show up and the Earl of Kildare was summoned back to England, charged with being a traitor, and held in the Tower of London for the next six years. In 1532, Gerait was again reinstated in Ireland, as many around Henry convinced him that it was to his political advantage to do so. However, in 1534, more charges were brought against him and he returned to the Tower of London for the last time. He died there.

His son, Lord Thomas (also known as "Silken Thomas"—for the silk scarves he and his followers wore), rebelled in Ireland, riding through the streets of Dublin with about 150 men declaring Irish Independence. At first he won a few battles, but then the English sent more troops, he was captured, hanged, drawn, and quartered, along with supposedly all the male members of his family. The English believed the Geraldine (or Fitzgerald) bloodline had been exterminated, and through the Act of Parliament in 1537, decreed all Geraldine lands were now forfeited to the Crown.

However, two children did in fact survive, and in one of them, Gerald Fitzgerald, then age twelve, Ireland would come to place her future hope. His aunt, Lady Eleanor Fitzgerald, secretly nursed and raised the boy, and then with great courage and conviction, united all the families of Ireland, both Gael and Shan Gall (the new foreign settlers), into a vast confederacy against the English. All past tribal conflicts and political disagreements were put aside and Ireland hoped by the beginning of the Seventeenth Century to virtually live as one nation, united in a common language, literature, religion, custom, music, and suffering. Gerald was conveyed to France to assure his security, and when Henry VIII learned of this, he sent his best friend, Lord Leonard Gray, Deputy of Ireland, to the gallows for allowing the boy to escape.

The hope of Ireland rested in Gerald, and everywhere he went in France, Italy, and Spain he was praised, followed by cheering crowds, and proclaimed the "King of Ireland". He was given the finest education known, studying with the Bishop of Verona among others. He was courted by all of Europe's leaders, including the Holy Roman Emperor, Charles V, and the new Pope, Paul III. It seemed not too many people cared for the English and King Henry VIII.

The French, Scots, and Irish were preparing for an invasion to liberate Ireland when the English, recognizing this, proposed the marriage of Mary Queen of Scots to their king-to-be, Edward VI, (which was basically accomplished by force) and at the last minute this symbolically united these two countries, Scotland and England. The French and Irish were originally hoping that Gerald was going to wed Mary. About this same time, the French King Francis I died, and Henry II became King of France. He had wanted Mary to wed his son. Consequently, all invasion plans were abandoned.

Gerald then subjected himself to Mary and petitioned her to reinstate his lands and title, which she did in part. These would then again be the center of various Irish revolts and rebellions, with Gerald as the leader and hero. Unfortunately, by this time the English had employed heavy artillery, the "Great Gray Guns", and the Irish could not match this weaponry.

King Edward VI, son of Henry VIII and Jane Seymour, Henry's third wife (Anne Boleyn was executed in 1536 for alleged treason and adultery), died in 1553, and was succeeded by Mary I, daughter of Henry VIII and his first wife Catherine of Aragon. Mary was an avid Catholic. Edward had tried to place Lady Jane Grey, a protestant, on the throne but she only lasted a few days, was overthrown and beheaded. Mary I tried to restore Catholicism with the same brutal violence that her father had used to promote Anglican Protestantism. She executed at least three hundred of the Protestant leaders (burning them at the stake) and sent hundreds more scurrying into exile in Germany, Switzerland, and in the case of John Knox, into Scotland. From there they plotted the restoration of Protestant England, and inspired a hatred of Catholicism that remains in many to this very day.

Mary's reign offered a welcomed reprieve and respite for Ireland, but it did not last long. When Mary married the Catholic Spanish Prince Philip (later to become King Philip II of Spain), her days were numbered. Following Mary's death in 1558, her half-sister, Elizabeth I, daughter of Henry VIII and Anne Boleyn, became Queen of England. Elizabeth I had previously been declared illegitimate by her father Henry, but nonetheless she resumed her father's policies (she apparently was never bothered also by the fact that he had beheaded her mother). Her violent treatment and attempted extermination of the Irish are well documented, as is evidenced by the fact that she demanded the heads of Irish Rebels, such as that of Shane O'Neill, as well as the heads of Irish Priests, be brought to her for examination, and then impaled and placed on display in Dublin, London and elsewhere.

There were countless acts of brutality and slaughter documented during the reigns of Henry VIII, Edward VI, and Elizabeth I, as well as horrific laws enacted by the English Parliament that called for the extermination of the Irish, who were quite often not even considered humans. And consequently, there was always the underlying current of Irish rebellion and desire for independence, personified in the great Irish heroes, such as Shane O'Neill, Hugh O'Neill, Hugh O'Donnell (also known as "Red Hugh"), and Rory O'Moore among others.

Shane O'Neill was descended from the High Kings of Ireland and was the chieftain of Tyrone in northwest Ulster. He was also known as "Shane the Proud". When his father, Conn the Lame, accepted the English title of Baron of Dungannon, Shane went into rebellion. Upon his father's deathbed he killed his half-brother whom would have become the new Baron, and reclaimed the lands for the Irish. He was an excellent soldier and won several battles over the English. Queen Elizabeth tried everything to subdue him. She even attempted to act as if she would honor him, acknowledge his claims, and make friends with him. She then attempted to poison him and his entire family, but the one administering the poison was unskilled and they all lived. Shane then knew with whom he dealt and became ever more determined.

*Trinity College Dublin. It was founded by Queen Elizabeth I in 1591-1592
and has produced many of the world's great literary figures including
Jonathan Swift, George Berkeley, Oliver Goldsmith, Edmund Burke, Thomas
Moore, Standish O'Grady, Oscar Wilde, Bram Stoker, James Joyce (UCD),
and Samuel Beckett.*

Queen Elizabeth sent three hundred English soldiers and several hundred mercenaries against Shane, who proceeded to kill them all. The English soldiers had worn these new scarlet coats into battle, and this battle was ever after called the "Battle of the Red Coats". In 1567, Shane was invited to a banquet given by Sorley Boy McDonnell, another Ulster nobleman whom Shane had once defeated. Queen Elizabeth and her Lord Deputy, Sussex, planted an assassin at the banquet and when all the men became drunk, he killed Shane and cut off his head. His head was then taken to Queen Elizabeth and later impaled and displayed upon the northwest gate of Dublin Castle.

Hugh O'Neill and Hugh O'Donnell (Red Hugh) formed an alliance in the last years of the Sixteenth Century that led to the "Nine Years' War" (1592-1601) and the near complete expulsion of the English from Ulster. Hugh O'Neill was born in County Tyrone in 1550, and was originally loyal to Queen Elizabeth I after she became queen in 1558. He was named Earl of Tyrone in 1587. He became "The O'Neill" in 1593, allowing him the capabilities of uniting the Irish Gaelic chieftains, which he did with great proficiency. In 1595 they destroyed an English fort and drove the English from the region of County Armagh.

Hugh O'Donnell had been the heir to the lands of the Tir-Conaill and was captured by the English at the age of fourteen and held in the Tower of Birmingham at Dublin Castle along with the two sons of Shane O'Neill, Henry and Art. They made a daring escape in the dead of winter, but Art and Henry both died from exposure. It was then that Red Hugh united with Hugh O'Neill and fought the Nine Years' War, which eventually drove most of the English from Ulster. A Treaty was proposed in 1602 that restored to the Irish their lands, but according to accounts Queen Elizabeth died an insane raving maniac in 1603 before the treaty could be signed, although she had agreed to do so. While on a trip to Spain, Red Hugh O'Donnell was poisoned by an agent of the English Lord Deputy. Hugh O'Neill was betrayed and accused of treason by the English as they placed a bounty on his life. He was forced to flee from Ireland in 1607 along with approximately fifty to ninety other Irish noblemen and chieftains, in an exodus that has come to be known as the "Flight of the Earls".

Rory O'Moore was the chief man responsible for the "Rising of 1641" in Ulster that led to the rumors of the "Popish Massacre". This will all be discussed further in the next lecture.

The Sixteenth Century was also the period of the Protestant Reformation and the English monarchy made every effort to force the Irish to accept their new protestant religion, including the closing of all Catholic churches and the confiscation of their properties; and, the mandated murdering of Priests. But the Irish, with their deeply spiritual and academic religious history, were never going to recognize the murderous and treacherous Henry or Elizabeth as the head of their church.

The Seventeenth Century

The Seventeenth Century began with the full-blown rebellion led by Hugh O'Neill and Red Hugh O'Donnell mentioned in the last lecture, the "Nine Years' War", at first showing quite favorably for the Irish. It was for the Irish a war of both independence and religion, and the Irish looked to the then greatest Catholic nation on earth for assistance, Spain. The aforementioned Hugh O'Neill in Ulster and Red Hugh O'Donnell in Connacht, were winning regularly against the English, basically through the use of superior tactics and strategies, and expelling the English from area after area.

In 1599, O'Neill took control of Armagh, and with it, Ulster. For allowing this to happen, Queen Elizabeth, beheaded one of her favorite and most capable generals, and courtier, Lord Essex. Most of the remaining English troops were now located in Munster, exactly where the Spanish reinforcements made landfall, at Kinsale. O'Neill had told the Spanish to make landfall in Ulster with at least five thousand men. They only brought three thousand and were under the command of a general, named d'Aquila, with somewhat questionable capabilities. They were immediately surrounded by the English and lost a battle they should have easily won—a battle that would have most likely assured Irish Independence. The Battle of Kinsale in 1601 is still viewed as a major turning point in the struggle for independence, a fact quite evident in this small seaside community famous for its gourmet restaurants.

O'Neill had fought his way south in an attempt to reach the Spanish, now he had to fight his way back to Ulster, fighting all the way in unfamiliar territory. His army had been in reality quite devastated, yet the English weren't aware of this and in fact proposed a treaty, restoring his and other Irish lands in 1602. Before the treaty could be signed however, Queen Elizabeth died on 23 March 1603, a raving madwoman according to accounts.

King James VI of Scotland, son of Lord Darnley and Mary Stuart, Queen of Scots (he had become King of Scotland in 1583 upon the abdication of his mother as Queen), then became King James I of England, and refused to both sign the treaty and restore Irish lands. He then circulated a forged document, purportedly written by O'Neill, which claimed O'Neill and his followers were planning another rebellion that would eventually overthrow the entire English monarchy. Every English Lord promised an army and O'Neill knew that their struggle was for now lost and his only safety, and that of his followers, was in fleeing to America or the European continent, where they would be welcomed in Spain, Rome, Brussels, and elsewhere. He also knew there were numerous Irish soldiers in the service of these countries, and perhaps he could raise an army that would eventually return to Ireland and secure independence.

In Irish history this is known as the "Flight of the Earls", and ushers in another very dark period. The leaders of many of the old Irish royal families left in 1607, most settling in France, Spain, and Rome where they were treated like royalty by Pope Paul V. When Hugh O'Neill died in 1616, he was given a royal funeral and buried in the Church of San Pietro on the Janiculum Hill, a site historically reserved for only the most prestigious of royalty.

Within a decade following the Flight of the Earls, King James devised a plan that has influenced Irish life to this very day. It was the development of the "Ulster Plantation". James decreed that all lands belonging to the Earls that had left now belonged to the English crown. James actually had a twofold purpose for doing this, as well as wanting to assure an English presence and control of this troublesome region of Ireland, he also wanted to get rid of several troublesome families in England. James I was never very popular with the English Lords, especially those known as the Presbyterian dissenters, because of his continuing efforts to form an alliance with long-time rival Spain; and, because of his strong belief in the "Divine Right of Kings". He gave many of these dissenters the acreage in Ireland. In reality these lands never had belonged to any of the individuals, but belonged to the entire tuath, or clan community, but they were now deeded over to England. Over four-million acres were confiscated, and re-deeded to English settlers in mostly one-thousand and two-thousand acre plots, and the true Irish owners were either driven off or murdered. It has been documented that many Irish were forced at this time to live like animals in the woods, feeding on leaves, roots, and berries. Many of these displaced tenants and landowners also fled to the European continent and America. During this period of the seventeenth century there was a substantial migration of Irish into present day North Carolina, South Carolina, Georgia, and somewhat Virginia (Virginia was a bit more English—remember it was given by Queen Elizabeth to one of her court-iers, Sir Walter Raleigh, who then named it for his "virgin" queen). This was also the period when the American pilgrims were coming to "New England" to attain religious freedom and relief from English oppression.

As I'm certain you're all well aware by now, the Irish were not about to lie down, starve to death, and die in the bogs. The Irish wrath and displeasure with the British were growing daily. James I died in 1625, and his son and successor Charles I then again outlawed Catholicism in 1641 and the Irish were again forced to worship and study in secrecy. It was during this period that the first of a long line of Irish secret societies was formed. It was known as the "Defenders", and was organized and led by Rory O'Moore" (also known as Roger Moore). Their secret password, or phrase, was "God, Our Lady, and Rory O'Moore".

The "Rising of 1641" was most probably the natural outcome of the accumu-lated effects of these Royal injustices and oppressive measures. It was also orga-nized mostly through the efforts of Rory O'Moore, from County Offaly, whom for many years had secretly and patiently worked to unite the Irish families and the exiled Irish soldiers and officers in an effort to overthrow the British and drive them from Ireland forever. He had lived in Spain for a number of years, where he most probably learned and perfected the art of organized revolution. The Rising was planned to overwhelm the transplanted British of Ulster on the night of 21 October 1641, and that is exactly what it did. The British landholders were forced to flee into the few walled cities they could hold, basically Derry, Belfast, and Enniskillen, and in one night the Irish pretty much reclaimed the entire province.

Unfortunately, only Ulster rose up that night. The original plans called for volunteer armies in the other provinces to do the same. The armies led by O'Moore, Macguire and MacMahon were supposed to overtake Dublin Castle, but these plans were revealed to the English by a traitor; and, Macguire and Mac-Mahon were killed and Rory O'Moore barely escaped.

Current research indicates very few English were killed during the Rising, probably mostly only those who had brought it on through their own particular actions. Most families were simply told to leave the Irish lands. But in the years following, fantastic stories developed outlining the atrocities of the great "Popish Massacre". The death toll kept mounting. The poet Milton, Cromwell's Secre-

tary at the time, eventually wrote that 610,000 English had been brutally slaughtered by the "Catholics" (there were only approximately 200,000 English residing
in the entirety of Ulster). Ten years after the Rising, the Cromwell Commission
conducted hearings, and protestant ministers one after another testified to the
slaughter they had witnessed. Most of these, it was later discovered, had not even
been present, or even in Ulster. Note: Similar testimony was given in the original
Bloody Sunday hearings in 1972, which were reopened in 1998. The "Irish Massacre of 1641" has even been perpetuated in numerous historical texts, when in
fact it has been shown to be in reality purely fiction. At the time, however, it was
politically advantageous for the Puritans to promote tales of such horrendous
atrocities. This became fuel for Cromwell and his New Model Army who would
soon kill and butcher thousands in the name of the Lord.

Two factions of the English parliament had been at odds for some time. In
November 1641, parliament issued Charles I with a list of over two hundred
grievances against the crown, known as the "Grand Remonstrance". Charles then
dissolved the parliament after invading it with soldiers on horseback and arresting
five of the leading members of the House of Commons. In 1642, the English parliamentary forces split and the English Civil War ensued, between Charles' "Cav-
aliers" and the Puritan "Roundheads". In 1646, the Roundheads won and in
1649 executed Charles I, at the fervent insistence of Oliver Cromwell, who
signed the King's Death Warrant (there's no doubt he liked killing). Cromwell
then declared himself "Lord Protector" of England. He also bestowed upon himself the titles of "Commander-In-Chief", and "Lord Lieutenant of Ireland"; and,
in 1649, he left for Ireland with his extremely modern and efficient "New Model
Army" to avenge the atrocities of the "Popish Massacre".

The Irish had no defense for this ultra-modern, super-efficient, state-of-the-art
killing machine. Cromwell and his men would be remembered in Ireland for all
time! This army went first to Drogheda where they killed over three thousand
soldiers and another thousand-plus townspeople, including women, children,
and the elderly, who had sought shelter in and around the church. Cromwell's
army basically wiped out the entire town of Drogheda. They went next to Wexford where they did the same thing, killing over two thousand. After Drogheda,
Cromwell wrote to the parliament, "It has pleased God to bless our endeavor at
Drogheda...I wish that all honest hearts may give the glory of this to God alone,
to whom indeed the praise of this mercy belongs." Parliament declared 2 October
1649, as a day of Thanksgiving in honor of the great victory.

Cromwell failed on his first attempt to capture Waterford, and not wanting to waste the time, he moved on to Cork city, a much easier prey, mainly because, according to accounts, a large number of English protestants lived there (probably many of those settling out following the Nine Years War and Battle of Kinsale) and they handed the remainder of the city over to Cromwell. The best fight against Cromwell was displayed at Clonmel, where Hugh O'Neill, son of the aforementioned Hugh O'Neill, with only 1500 men, allowed Cromwell to enter the town, where the O'Neill forces surrounded them and killed over five-hundred of Cromwell's soldiers. Cromwell never could then capture the city after several attempts, and had to resort to a blockade, during which O'Neill's men a few at a time slipped away at night until they were all out of the city.

As well as these major cities, Cromwell's army destroyed scores of smaller towns and villages along their routes. Another aspect of their strategy or tactics was to destroy all the crops along the way hoping to starve those who remained. The army had with them large numbers of scythes and cut down, then burned, all the crops. In eight months, Cromwell had devastated a good portion of the island. In May 1650, he returned to England.

He left an army in Ireland, under the command of at first general Henry Ireton (who married Cromwell's daughter in 1646) and then upon his death during a siege of Limerick in 1651, Cromwell's son Richard Henry took over. The cities that had not been conquered, such as Kilkenny, Waterford, Galway, and Limerick, had negotiated "settlements", and on 12 May 1652, the controversial "Articles of Kilkenny"(basically signed by two pro-English factions) were signed putting an end to probably the worst period in all of Ireland's rather tragic history.

Although most of the killing was ended, the suffering of the Irish People was far from over. Through what is known as the "Cromwellian Settlement", all Irish lands east of the River Shannon were forfeited to the English, and the Irish were ordered to "Hell or Connacht" (by act of Parliament and under penalty of death, no Irish person was to be found east of the Shannon River after 1 May, 1654). The land in Connacht is the worst agriculturally in all of Ireland, containing more rocks than soil. Cromwell himself made the comment that in Connacht there was, "not enough wood to hang a man, not enough water to drown a man, and not enough soil to cover his corpse". This again stimulated a major migration—to the armies, trade guilds, and universities of continental Europe, and again also to America.

The Cromwellian settlement was facilitated mostly through the work of one William Petty, a renowned statistician, scientist, and fervent Protestant and hater of Catholics. He completed a comprehensive survey of land ownership in Ireland, in both record time and with unbelievable accuracy. Following his work, Ireland had the dubious distinction of being the most accurately and thoroughly mapped country in all of Europe. The work of Irish dispossession was accomplished just as rapidly and efficiently. All Irish lands east of the Shannon River were confiscated and most were then deeded to Cromwell's soldiers, or to other Englishmen who had financially supported Cromwell's efforts in Ireland and elsewhere. Some of the land was also given to the English clergy and schoolmasters for the purpose of establishing Protestant churches and schools. In the long term however, the main benefactors were to become the Irish Protestant ascendancy landlords of the following two hundred years, as they often bought the lands for almost nothing from the Cromwellian soldiers, who had no intention of living permanently in Ireland. Most of the massive estates with their great houses were established from this period.

As if this all wasn't enough, the plague hit Ireland in 1652 and 1653, probably due, at least in part, to the carnage and decay. Following this period various historians have estimated that between two-thirds and five-sixths of the Irish population had been either exterminated, or had left the country. Even after all this, the Irish People survived, revived, and came back even stronger. Cromwell died in 1658.

In 1660, Charles II, son of Charles I, was asked to return to the throne from his exile in France amid great rejoicing. Most of the English were tired of the staunch, "holier-than-thou", and extremely judgmental and oppressive attitudes of the Puritans. The King's right hand man and long time friend was a fellow named James Butler, the Duke of Ormond, who had been in exile in France along with Charles, and was placed in charge of the resettlement of Irish lands. Those older landowners, both Catholic and Protestant, who had also either been in exile with, or remained in great favor with Charles II were immediately restored to their lands. These were rather small in number. Butler, it has been said, was basically in favor of a complete reversal of the Cromwellian settlement, but when it was discovered that concessions towards Catholics would cause a violent political backlash among Protestants in England, he backed off from complete reversal and instead suggested to the King that with minor modifications, the Cromwellian settlement should stand in Ireland. This of course proved extremely disappointing to the dispossessed Catholic landowners who had hoped to receive favor from both the King and the Duke of Ormond.

The only tangible improvement in the lives of Catholics following the Stuart restoration was the welcomed relief from the extremely harsh and intense religious persecution of Cromwell and the Puritans. The Catholic clergy, most of which had fled to the European continent, were allowed to return and again resume their work in Ireland. However, there were still the occasional outbreaks of violence and oppression, such as the murder of Oliver Plunkett, Archbishop of Armagh.

Oliver Plunkett was an extremely learned man and one of great peace. He studied for the priesthood in Rome at the Irish College that had been founded by Luke Wadding. He returned to Ireland upon his appointment as Archbishop of Armagh. In 1879 he was falsely accused of participation in a "Popish Plot" that was to land French troops in Ireland and initiate the overthrow of the English monarchy. He was imprisoned in Dublin Castle but his Irish trial had to be abandoned because no credible witnesses could be found. The following year he was taken to London and imprisoned in Newgate Jail. Upon the testimony of several "questionable" witnesses he was convicted and sentenced to death in 1681. On 1 July of that year he was hanged, drawn and quartered in Tyburn, England. His final words called for forgiveness of all those participating.

For over two centuries Oliver Plunkett's severed head was cared for by the Dominican nuns in Drogheda and is now on display at a shrine honoring him in St. Peter's Church on West Street in Drogheda, along with the door from his cell at Newgate. Oliver Plunkett was canonised by Pope Paul VI in St. Peter's Square on the twelfth of October 1975. In 1979, when Pope John Paul II visited Ireland, he made a pilgrimage to the shrine of Oliver Plunkett and praised the work of this great man of peace.

Anyway, back in England many of the staunch Puritans were still present in the parliament and battled with Charles II often, devising several "Popish Plots"(which were basically false rumors that the Queen and Irish Catholics were going to kill Charles, so his brother James, the Duke of York and a catholic, could take over the throne). The truth was that Charles was in fact considering a return of Catholic toleration to England, which actually led to a brief war with the Netherlands (1672-74) and once again dissolution of the English Parliament in 1681, after the Whigs tried to pass legislation that would forbid James from ever taking the throne. Well, the pro-Charles forces won out, many of the Puritans were arrested, executed, or exiled, and in 1685, upon the death of Charles II, the Protestants worst nightmare came true as James took the throne as King James II, but as we shall see, the battles were not yet over.

James II versus William of Orange:

When James II took the throne of England in 1685, one of his very first acts was to suspend the Penal Laws. He was a Catholic and this act struck terror in the hearts of the Puritans and Protestant England. They well remembered the earlier actions of Mary I, as she sought vengeance for the atrocities that had been perpetuated against Catholics by burning several Protestant leaders at the stake. They also of course still believed in the horrors of the "Popish Massacre". James had married Anne Hyde in 1659, the mother of two future Queens Mary II (1688-1694) and Anne (1702-1714). She died in 1671 and James married Mary of Modena. She became Catholic and she gave birth to James Edward Stuart, latterly to be known as "The Pretender".

James appointed Richard Talbot the "Duke of Tyrconnell" and sent him to oversee affairs in Ireland. He was a large powerful man who had been at Drogheda, a lad of sixteen, when Cromwell came through. He immediately removed all Puritans from the ranks of the military and replaced them, both officers and soldiers, with Irish Catholics. Three thousand of these Irish Catholic soldiers were sent to England to reinforce James' army there. Their arrival in England was met with horror and panic.

English Protestant agents began communicating with one William III of Orange, head of the House of Orange in the Netherlands, who had a double bloodline connection to the English throne, as he was married to his cousin Mary, James II's eldest daughter, an avid Protestant, and both were grandchildren of Charles I. Louis XIV in France sent messengers to James advising him that he should beware of these communications. James actually resented the accusations of Louis XIV because, after all, William was married to James' daughter.

In 1688, James' wife gave birth to a son (James Edward Stuart), thus assuring a Catholic heir and ascendancy to the throne. This was more than the English Protestants could bare, and they invited William of Orange to invade England and overthrow the monarchy of James II. In November 1688, William arrived in England and met virtually no opposition. James' army melted away, his friends and family deserted him and William was welcomed with a great celebration by the English people. This is known as the "Glorious Revolution", and James was forced to flee to the protection of Louis XIV in France.

William and Mary immediately acknowledged a "Bill of Rights" that limited the powers of the monarchy, assured the privileged status of the English elite, and prohibited any Roman Catholics from ever again ascending to the throne of England. In 1701, the "Act of Settlement" was drawn up which stated that if no heirs survived Anne, the second daughter of James and what would be the last of the Stuart monarchs, that the throne of England would be passed to the protestant German House of Hanover—and that is exactly what happened. When Queen Anne died in 1714, having outlived all of her children, the "Elector" of the House of Hanover became King George I of England—he was the third foreign monarch to ascend to the English throne in just over a century, two of which could not even speak English. George I never even visited England, considering it a wretched and disgusting country.

Most all Catholics, along with the Irish soldiers who had been sent to England scrambled back to Ireland and prepared for a fight. Another false rumor was being circulated in England claiming that the Irish were slaughtering Protestants in Ireland. It was becoming obvious that the dispute for the English crown between James and William was going to be settled on Irish soil. Within two months over fifty thousand Irishmen enlisted in the Irish army, led by Richard Talbot, the Duke of Tyrconnell. They were known by those in William's army as the "Irish Black Guard", a raggedy group with no uniforms, and many not even wearing shoes.

William Petty, the famous statistician who completed the land survey for Cromwell, was now Sir William Petty, and was now commissioned to complete a census in Ireland. His findings declared that there were one-million-three-hundred thousand inhabitants, most of whom were subsistent agriculturalists. Many of these supplemented their incomes through the spinning and weaving of wool and linen, which along with meat and butter, constituted the main exports of Ireland during this period. The English landlords at this time derived most of their income from rents and paid offices established by the English crown, and as the markets began to shrink so did the rents which would eventually lead to further conflict.

The Duke of Tyrconnell sent to France for James, declaring he must fight for the throne and this could best be accomplished from Ireland. James landed at Kinsale on the nineteenth of March 1689, with gold, arms, ammunition, and over four hundred French officers and sharpshooters. Tyrconnell met him at Cork and the combined armies marched northward, encountering basically no opposition on the march to Ulster, until they reached the town of Derry, where the city's apprentice boys slammed the city gates closed on James, screaming "no surrender". The siege of Derry lasted 109 days, during which time James became disgusted and went to Dublin. In Dublin, James was met with great enthusiasm, he partied heartily, an Irish parliament was established, and plans were finalized for a more aggressive assault on Ulster. At Derry, it's reported over one thousand died from starvation and dysentery during the siege and blockade, which is still the main rallying cry of the Orangemen to this very day.

William's army arrived at Belfast in late summer, under the command of the Dutch general, Schomberg, and proceeded to attack Carrickfergus, finally capturing it following a week's siege. They sailed up the River Foyle and broke the siege/blockade at Derry. They then established their camp at Dundalk. The autumn rains were coming, disease was ravaging William's army, and the French generals were advising James to attack at that time, however he did not agree and forbade the attack. He even accused the French generals of trying to usurp his command and James angrily returned to Dublin. In March 1690, William then sent seven thousand more troops to reinforce Schomberg. They also brought the first recently invented rapid-fire guns, capable of firing the equivalent of over 100 musket rounds per minute. In June, William came to join his troops, aware of the great importance of this struggle.

Meanwhile, James and his army abandoned their positions in the north which basically had William's armies surrounded, and retreated down the Boyne River. (It is said that James already had ships awaiting him at Waterford for the purpose of carrying him back to France, where he enjoyed the lavish lifestyle). The two armies met on 1 July 1690, with James' army inferior in both numbers (26,000 to over 36,000), and in weaponry.

The "Battle of the Boyne" raged all day with William's army slowly gaining ground. At five o'clock James fled for Dublin, arriving there at ten o'clock that night. At nightfall, the Irish army dissipated having no command, with the battle being fought virtually to a standstill. In Dublin, James stated that the Irish army had fled the battlefield and that he would never again lead an Irish army. He promptly then left for Waterford and sailed to France, never to again set foot on any Irish nor English soil.

The Irish however were determined to continue fighting, as their goal was far more important than the restoration of the Stuart monarchy. Their goal was Irish independence. The French generals wanted to seek favorable terms from William and then return to France. The bulk of the Irish army went to Limerick. The French general, Lauzun, went to Galway with the French soldiers and most of the guns and ammunition. William knew of the dissention and the French army's desire to return to France. He offered favorable terms to end the conflict.

The Irish had suffered far too greatly over the years behind the English promises of favorable terms. They were determined to never give in, prepared to die rather than yield. The Irish held out bravely through three sieges orchestrated by William's far more capable legions, and had even driven the English armies back into the bog following a victory by James' army at the Bridge of Athlone. Meanwhile the cities of Cork and Kinsale had fallen to the English.

There was only one hope left for the English in Limerick, and that was to attempt to break through at the narrow Aughrim Pass, and it was well defended by the Irish's superior position from the surrounding hills and from Aughrim Castle. As the English advanced, it was discovered that the cases of bullets and cannon balls left for the Irish were not compatible with their muskets and canons. They tore up everything they had made of metal in an effort to provide ammunition, even the buttons off their coats, but were in the end no match for the English's superior weaponry.

The English again offered terms, but Limerick refused to quit and William's army again attacked on 23 September 1690. When they could not overtake the city, they turned the siege into a blockade, and again offered "favorable terms" as they were anxious to return to England, promising the Irish many freedoms, including that of religion and the restoration of their lands. The Irish leader, Sarsfield, did not trust the English and demanded that the treaty be signed by the Lord Justices who had to come all the way from Dublin. They did so and placed their signatures upon the treaty. The Irish were guaranteed all the rights of citizens and were to be, "secure from any and all disturbances at the hands of the English".

The Treaty of Limerick was signed in 1691, although it was not approved by the English parliament until 1697, and then, in a seriously altered form. Irish officers and soldiers were given the choice of staying in Ireland, swearing an oath of allegiance to William, and living in peace; or, they would be allowed to leave the country. Over ninety-five percent elected to leave the country. This has come to be known historically as the "Flight of the Wild Geese". Many of these Irish officers and soldiers went on to distinguish themselves in armies and conflicts around the world.

The "faith and honour" of the British Crown were pledged to the Irish in the "Treaty of Limerick", yet within three years of its signing, the harshest of all Penal Laws and the most fervent of all persecutions against Catholics were begun in Ireland. The English Protestant clergy screamed from their pulpits about the "sins" of keeping faith with, and/or promises to, the Papists. There were still at this time, and for many years following, annual Anglican Church services celebrating the divine deliverance of the Protestants from the hands of the Catholics during the famed Popish Massacre of 1641.

Glenveagh Castle in County Donegal, home of the Earl of Leitrim.

The Eighteenth Century

The Penal Laws enacted following the Williamite Wars were the harshest and most brutal of any in recorded history. Furthermore they were quite unique in the fact that they were not directed at a religious minority, such as, for example, the Huguenots in France; but they were directed at the overwhelming majority of the population. Also, the aim was not to convert or force into exile the targets of their persecution, but to reduce the population to a status of ignorant impotent subservience. Every effort was made to disallow nine-tenths of the population to better themselves socially, intellectually, economically, or in any other way; and, their centuries-old culture was outlawed.

The fervent brutality became even worse after the German Hanoverians, beginning with George I, ascended to the English throne in 1714. To demonstrate the scope and intent of these penal laws—between 1695 and 1720, laws were enacted forbidding the Irish Catholics from any of the following:

> They were to own no gun, sword, knife, nor any weaponry.
> They were excluded from their country's parliament.
> They were excluded from their country's military.
> They could hold no government position, nor job.
> They could not enter the legal profession.
> They could not teach nor maintain schools.
> They could not send children abroad to be educated.
> They could not own nor buy land.
> They were prohibited from receiving land as a gift.
> They were forbidden to join any profession.
> They could not own a horse worth more than five pounds.
> They were forbidden from voting.
> Catholics were forbidden from inheriting anything from Protestants.
> They were not allowed to engage in international commerce (major factor).
> They could not be the guardian of, nor foster, a child.
> They could make no profit from their land exceeding 30% of rent.
> Upon the death of parents, no child could be left with Catholics.
> They could not attend any Catholic worship services.

Priests and catholic clergy were outlawed under penalty of death.
If an unhappy or unfaithful wife would become Protestant, she would then receive all of the family property.
They were forbidden from speaking the Irish language.
They could not listen to Irish music.
They could engage in no Irish customs.

These laws were designed to accomplish cultural genocide, and to eliminate Roman Catholics from Ireland; and, in effect by their wording ignored, or presupposed, that no such people even existed. What extreme arrogance! Furthermore, any magistrate could visit the house of any Irish Catholic, at any hour of the day or night, for the purpose of searching for weapons. One need only imagine the horrendous stories that came from these situations.

Catholic clergy were especially targeted. They were outlawed, and if anyone came upon one, he was obligated to kill him, or face being killed himself. They held mass, as well as educational classes, far out into the wilds, often around the natural springs that then became Holy Wells, with numerous sentries posted in an attempt to insure their safety. These became known as "hedge schools" or "hedge meetings", because the teachers and students often hid behind, or among, the hedges. Teachers and Clergy had to dress in rags and act stupid, and were still quite often discovered, usually betrayed by a paid informer, perhaps someone desperately needing the money to feed his or her family. If groups were discovered worshipping on the mountainside, quite often the entire group was slaughtered.

To insure that the Penal Laws were being enforced, the various counties had to issue annual "Returns" stating how many Catholics had been arrested, how many had died, and the numbers currently being held in jails and prisons. These have been preserved in the official state records and cast an interesting perspective on the Penal Laws. These laws were enforced all the way to the end of the Eighteenth Century, and led in part to the development of the "Volunteer" movement.

England attempted to wipe out Irish trade and industry with the same enthusiasm with which they sought to wipe out Catholicism. The Irish had been international traders and artisans for many centuries, with documented dealings going as far back as the Phoenicians. They were known throughout the world for their excellent agricultural products, art, craftsmanship, and weaving.

The woolen industry was booming at the time of the English occupation, and the English then mandated that the Irish could export woolen products to nowhere except England, and then at a very low price. They were still permitted however to produce and export hemp and linen. When the Irish developed these commodities into a profit-producing mode, these were then also outlawed by England. The Irish next turned to cattle and sheep. These were soon outlawed. Next came the production of cheese and butter (still considered among the finest in the world), and many in the English Parliament were annoyed at having to amend the laws to include these.

The Irish then began exporting butchered meat. This became outlawed. Next came the extremely fine glass industry (the Irish still produce arguably the world's finest crystal)—this was then outlawed. Next came fishing and fisheries, and these were also forbidden from exportation—all under the pretense that the enemies of Britain were in no way to be supplied with these things. Oh yes, I forgot about the silk industry that came to prominence in the middle of the Eighteenth Century, exportation of silk was again forbidden. Many historians argue that these measures were the most devastating of all to the Irish people, keeping them subservient and without an avenue to economic or political freedom for several generations. Many of these industries haven't recovered to this very day, basically because of a long-standing loss of market share.

It was inevitable that this sort of oppression would eventually again lead to an Irish Nationalist, or Republican-type, movement. The Irish were also well aware of the events taking place in America, and driven somewhat by the ideals of the French Revolution that were spreading throughout Europe. The American presentation of the Declaration of Independence on 4 July 1776 had a profound affect on a vast number of Irishmen. In April of 1778, the American John Paul Jones sailed into Belfast Harbor and in broad daylight sank a British Man-of-war ship. Shortly thereafter, the first corps of "Irish Volunteers" was formed in Belfast.

Confusion at an ancient Council meeting.

The British at this particular time were at war with America, France, Spain and Holland, and were not on particularly good terms with the heavily armed but neutral Russia and Scandanavian-regional coalition. There then came a serious threat of a French invasion of Ireland, and Britain had no available troops to commit to her defense. A French invasion may have been welcomed throughout the majority of Ireland, but the Protestant north, only a couple of generations removed from the memories of Mary I, and all the troubles we've just discussed, had no desire to fall under French and Papal domination. In November of 1778, a law was passed enabling Irish Catholics, after taking the Oath of Allegiance to the British crown, to own and/or lease property. This was an effort to secure loyalty and did tide over difficulties for a bit, but Ireland was in such desperate financial straits that there remained an underlying current of those seeking relief and independence.

One of those fighting to gain some relief, and the one responsible for an easing of some of the Irish trade restrictions; and, one of those most influential in the formation of an Irish Parliament, was a solicitor by the name of Henry Grattan. He was born in Dublin on the fourth of July in 1746. His father was for many years the Recorder for Dublin. Henry graduated from Trinity College, Dublin in 1767, and was admitted to Middle Temple University in London the same year to study law. During this period he spent a great deal of time at Westminster following the actions of the English Parliament, where he became especially taken with the work and oratory of Edmund Burke, another Dublin and Trinity College man. Henry Grattan's landlady often complained that he would walk around the garden at all hours of the night expounding arguments and screaming, "Mr. Speaker, I demand…"—imitating the speeches of Edmund Burke.

In 1772 he was called to the Irish Bar and in 1775 he entered the Irish Parliament in Dublin as an MP for the area of Charlemont in County Armagh. He quickly ascended to the head of the Patriot Party, nearly fighting a dual at one point with the man he replaced, Henry Flood. By 1779 he had persuaded the English government to reduce or remove many of the Irish trade restrictions and penal laws, and by 1782 had secured the short-lived "independence" of the Irish Parliament. The Irish Parliament even voted him a gratuity of fifty thousand pounds. His work and authority however were always undermined by the efforts of Henry Flood.

Henry Grattan urged political agitation and often stated, "The Irish Protestant should never be free until the Irish Catholic ceases to be a slave." He fought for Catholic emancipation unsuccessfully and retired from Parliament in 1797. He returned in 1800 wearing the uniform of the Volunteers to speak against the Act of Union, which was legislation binding Ireland to Great Britain. The beautiful development of Georgian Dublin also occurred during Grattan's stay in Parliament. Henry Grattan passed away on the fourth of June 1820 and is buried at Westminster Abbey.

Theobald Wolfe Tone and the United Irishmen:

The Irish had been dealing with the English for quite some time now and had learned a great deal about their ways. The Irishmen were becoming wiser and more realistic; and, were beginning to realize that their only hope rested in knowledge, unity, and at the very least arming themselves against the English invaders and oppressors. By 1780, the "Irish Volunteers" numbered over 100,000 armed and disciplined men. They were led and trained by officers that had learned their trade in some of the finest armies of Europe. They had actually begun as an effort of the city of Belfast to raise troops able to respond to the perceived threat of a French invasion. The Volunteer movement quite rapidly spread throughout Ireland, and became formally organized into brigades, artillery corps, and various specialized troops. The Volunteer movement was feared by Dublin Castle, but not nearly as much as a French invasion. At one point the British government even provided the Irish Volunteers with twenty thousand muskets, most of them distributed to Irish Catholics who were prohibited by law from even owning any type of weapon.

The American experience and the redress of the intolerable evils, especially those involving the trade embargoes, suffered by the Irish at the hands of the English soon became the main topics of both political and parlor discussions. The first step proposed in meetings called by the Volunteers was a movement calling for the non-importation, or boycotting, of all English goods. The Irish would only eat, wear, and utilize goods produced in Ireland. The Volunteers were to see that the embargo was obeyed, warning merchants and shopkeepers of possible severe consequences for not doing so. This was a fairly bold and quite effective measure. The Volunteers were extremely valuable in assisting the Parliamentary efforts of those like Henry Grattan.

In October 1779, a bill was introduced into the Irish Parliament calling for "Free Trade" for Ireland, allowing Ireland to import and export whatever products she so desired. In front of Trinity College, Napper Tandy had located his Irish Volunteers and their artillery cannons pointed at the Parliament Building (now the Bank of Ireland), along with a placard that read "Free Trade or _____". Within a couple of weeks the embargo of, and exportation restrictions placed on, Irish goods were removed.

All appeared as if it was going well, but the truth of the matter was that the Irish Parliament was still under the restrictions imposed by the Poynings Act, and was in fact a puppet of the English parliament. On the nineteenth of October 1781, Cornwallis surrendered to the Americans at Yorktown, and the English parliament became quite fearful and relatively certain that the Irish would attempt to follow suit and seek independence. They began planning methods to which Ireland would be permanently tied to England, while at the same time the Volunteers were planning ways to severe this relationship.

I've mentioned previously the Poynings Act, which stated that the Irish Parliament could only deal with laws and legislation that the English parliament directed it to address or consider. In addition to this act, there was also the "Declaratory Act", also known as the "Sixth Act of George I", penned in 1719. This Act declared that the king of England also had the "full power and authority to make laws and statutes of sufficient force and validity to bind the people and the Kingdom of Ireland." The Irish Volunteers had steadily gained power and support for the Irish causes from 1779 to 1782; and, had become the only important political force in the all of Ireland. Following the events in America, there was a bill rushed through the English Parliament repealing the Declaratory Act in 1782, with the announcement made shortly thereafter in the Irish Parliament.

In theory, Ireland was constitutionally liberated and a bloodless revolution had been successful. The Irish Volunteers then convened a National Convention on 10 November 1783 to discuss reform measures and the reorganization of the Irish Parliament. One hundred and fifty thousand armed men showed up and the primary order of business was Catholic emancipation, with the Parliament fairly evenly divided on this issue. The Convention ultimately rejected Catholic emancipation by a very narrow margin, and several influential Volunteers began drifting to the Parliamentary position. Soon the Volunteer movement was in shambles. It became something of a Parliament versus the Catholics argument and in response to the mostly Catholic Volunteer organization there came into existence the Protestant Peep-o'-Day Boys in Ulster and they began waging terrorist campaigns against Catholics, claiming to have driven over seven thousand Catholics out of County Armagh alone.

There was a young counselor, or solicitor, by the name of Theobald Wolfe Tone who spent as much time as possible setting in the gallery in the Irish House of Commons. Wolfe Tone was born on Stafford Street (now Wolfe Tone Street) in Dublin on the twentieth of June 1763. He graduated from Trinity College, Dublin and was called to the Irish Bar in 1789, but his true love was always politics. He was one of the first to write about the fact that these laws binding the Irish Parliament, as well as the connection with England, were at the root of the Irish people's problems. In 1790, he wrote, "That the influence of England was the radical vice of our Government, and that Ireland would never either be free, prosperous, or happy, until she was independent, and that independence was unattainable whilst the connection with England existed". England wanted it to appear through the repeal of the Declaratory Act that Ireland had been given its freedom, but Tone, Grattan, and others recognized that this was not the case.

Tone pointed to three main defects in this "independence". First, was the clause in the Constitution of 1782, that this "Irish Independence", "united Britain and Ireland under one Sovereign". This didn't sound of Irish independence. It then further stated that this "independence", "annexed the crown of Ireland inseparably to the crown of Great Britain". Secondly, Wolfe Tone noted that over three-quarters of the Irish population had no representation in this "Irish Parliament". Catholics, who made up over three-fourths of the Irish population, could neither sit in, nor vote for a member of this Parliament. And thirdly, that this Irish Parliament, even as an instrument of the Protestant minority, was totally inept, corrupt, and unrepresentative of any important Irish interests.

One day while viewing the follies of the Irish House of Commons, Tone met a young soldier, Captain Thomas Russell, and a lifelong friendship ensued. These two, and eventually several other like-minded individuals, began meeting at Tone's home in Irishtown, a Dublin suburb, and discussing such topics as the French and American revolutions, and the current oppressed, enslaved, and out-cast conditions of both the Irish Catholics, and the Presbyterian Dissenters. Tone's group saw a need to unite these two factions, as both were severely disen-franchised. It may be interesting to note that there were many more revolutionary influences and points of view considered and discussed at this time as well, such as those of the Jacobins of the French Revolution, and the Illuminati, founded by Weisshaupt in Bavaria in 1776 (but by 1782 had found its way into the political discussions throughout Europe). These both believed in total revolution and the overthrow of all forms of government and all creeds of religion. They advocated unbridled sensual pleasure with no restrictions set upon the individual by ethics nor morality, and considered patriotism and loyalty narrow-minded and inhibit-ing the growth of universal brotherhood. These ideas also influenced the Carbon-ari of the early nineteenth century in Italy, who with Mazzini's "Young Italy" movement helped unify current Italy.

Tone then wrote a pamphlet in 1791 entitled, "An Argument On Behalf of the Catholics of Ireland" and sent it to the Presbyterian Dissenters. He signed it "A Northern Whig", however his authorship was never really a secret, and in it he outlined the fact that these two groups had "one common interest and one com-mon enemy". Out of this was formed the idea of a political action party of united Irishmen; and, on the Eighteenth of October 1791, the first general meeting of the "United Irishmen" was held. Many former members of the Irish Volunteers were present, as were northern Presbyterians, and Theobald's concept was to include and unite all elements of the Irish people, stating he wished to "substitute the common name of Irishman, in the place of the denominations of Protestant, Catholic and Dissenter". Three resolutions were passed at this meeting:

1. The weight of English influence in the Government of Ireland was so great that it required a cordial union among all the people of Ireland in order to maintain that balance which is essential to the preservation of all individuals' liberties, and the extension, growth and preservation of commerce.

2. The sole constitutional avenue by which this English influence may be opposed is by initiating complete and radical reform measures regarding the methods of elected representation of those serving in the Irish Parliament.

3. That no reform is just nor proper which does not include Irishmen of every religious persuasion.

The United Irishmen were, as previously mentioned, first founded in Belfast as basically a debating society interested in parliamentary reform, but within a year there was a well-organized branch active in Dublin also. A prominent figure in this group was Napper Tandy (he served as secretary), the fellow who had earlier trained his cannons on the House of Parliament. He was the primary disseminator of information between revolutionary France and the Irish groups. In early 1792, the newspaper, *The Northern Star*, under the editorship of Samuel Neilson, was founded in Belfast and the *Evening Star* was founded in Dublin, to expound the views of the United Irishmen.

Eventually, England would employ every tactic imaginable to crush the United Irishmen, and from 1793 onward the United Irishman would become much more of a secret society. England was extremely fearful of this building coalition between Catholics and Protestants. In 1793, the Catholic Relief Bill was passed and it soon became evident that the British government was planning a policy of dividing the Catholic and Protestant factions. The United Irishmen and their publications exposed, and were very critical of, this policy of division; and, in 1784 the British government acted vigorously to stamp out the organization and their publications. Laws known as the "Convention Acts" were passed that forbade Irishmen from holding or attending any public meetings. Police and magistrates were allowed to invade and smash to pieces any house, office, or newspaper that was suspected of having United Irishmen sympathies. The United Irishmen were then reorganized into a more revolutionary secret nationalistic society, organized by province and drafting new policies and oaths of secrecy.

In 1794 the French sent a cleric by the name of William Jackson to Ireland for the purpose of assessing for the French government the methods that should be employed for an invasion. Theobald Wolfe Tone had written for Jackson a memorandum of introduction, and when Jackson was betrayed and arrested, Wolfe Tone became a marked man. He narrowly escaped arrest and immigrated to America in 1795.

At this time also, in 1795, the Orange Society (later to become the Orange Order) was formed (basically along the lines of Freemasonry). It became an extremely secretive, violent, and bigoted organization whose main goal was to crush the United Irishmen, and intimidate these once fair-minded individuals whose only wish was to include all Irishmen in a positive-minded effort to better Ireland. They claimed responsibility for driving every Catholic out of County Armagh, where the organization originated, and then confiscated all Catholic property, almost exclusively through the use of intimidation and violence. Catholic churches were burned and the violence soon spread to counties Down, Derry, Antrim and Tyrone. This only drove people to more actively embrace the United Irishmen, and their spin-off group, the Society of Defenders, who were organized to counter the efforts of the Orange Society and the Peep-o'-Day Boys. The most notable confrontation between these groups occurred on 21 September 1795, and is known as the "Battle of the Diamond". It was pretty much a standoff until the British military showed up and sided with the Orange Society coalition, killing several members of The Society of Defenders, and setting the tone for future events. The Peep-o'-Day Boys had been pretty much an organization from the lower classes, but the Orange Society began attracting more influential and affluent northern Protestants. This heightened French interest in the cause of Irish independence.

Following approximately four years of purely constitutional efforts, the United Irishmen, who had by now absorbed the Society of Defenders into their midst (largely through the efforts of Napper Tandy) remodeled themselves along military lines, realizing this was the only way Ireland could defend herself sufficiently, and achieve any sort of freedom. Looking again to the examples of France and America, Tone visited both these in an effort to secure their assistance. In 1796, Wolfe Tone had convinced the French to assist, and an expedition to free Ireland was initiated. It left Brest, France in December of 1796. It was to land at Bantry Bay on the southwest coast of Ireland, but at the appointed time, the weather was so bad (consisting of a series of storms that scattered the ships dramatically), that the French fleet was unable to land and hence it returned to

France. There is currently a museum and memorial at Bantry Bay commemorating this expedition.

Following the failure of the Bantry Bay expedition, more and more people believed that the United Irishmen should rise up on their own and not rely on foreign aid. Hence, the "Rising of 1798" was organized. The English government became aware of this action and initiated an elaborate campaign of paid informers that were to infiltrate as deeply as possible the inner workings of the United Irishmen. Wolfe Tone was back in France and had received a commitment of limited French aid. The informers learned just enough to identify the leaders of the Rising and their tentative plans, and just before the planned Rising, many of the leaders were arrested and killed, throwing a great deal of the plan into disarray. The small French fleet, including also Wolfe Tone aboard the battleship *Hoche*, was surrounded and captured in Lough Swilly on the County Donegal coast on the twelfth of October.

Tone was dressed in a French officer's uniform and was extremely proficient in the French language. At first he was not detected and simply detained with the other prisoners at Letterkenny, but then was recognized by a British officer who had attended Trinity College with Theobald, and he was taken prisoner. Wolfe Tone was given the sentence to be hung as a traitor. He requested to be executed as a soldier by firing squad, but when this was denied, he took his own life and died on the Nineteenth of November 1798.

The British themselves realized that the focus of much of the Irish discontent was the extremely incapable and corrupt "Irish" Parliament. To alleviate this problem England sought to devise a method of bringing Ireland directly under the control of the English parliament. William Pitt the Younger had become the Tory Prime Minister in 1783 and he was convinced that this was absolutely necessary to avoid further rebellion in Ireland. This Pitt and others decided would be done through an "Act of Union". They knew they couldn't just thrust such a thing upon the Irish—they had to make it appear that the Irish wanted this union. The English then devised one of the most elaborate schemes of bribery, intimidation, and extortion the world has ever seen. They needed signatures—on petitions that favored the political union of Ireland and England.

They had learned previously that certain of the extremely poor and hungry Irish people could be bribed. These were immediately paid for their signatures.

Next, it became a requirement to sign the petition as a prerequisite to holding any government job or position; and, not only must you sign the petition, but so must all of your relatives—for three generations. All avenues of government patronage were employed to secure signatures. The English clergy became involved and preached from their pulpits about the necessity of signing the petition. Of course the Orange Order was still active in the areas of violence and intimidation. Those brave enough to stand up for their independence and their rights, were abused and persecuted in extremely harsh ways, both publicly and privately.

In Parliament session after Parliament session the Act of Union was introduced and defeated. The English government then reapportioned legislative districts and actually paid these districts to send the desired candidates to Parliament. Finally, by August of 1800, enough votes were gathered to pass the Act of Union. It took effect on 1 January 1801, and united Ireland and England into "The United Kingdom of Great Britain and Ireland". Historians have estimated that in excess of 8000 pounds was paid for each vote, and of all the votes cast for the Act of Union (162), only seven were not paid a bribe. Also, out of the over three hundred members of Parliament, it is believed that possibly only seventy-two were legitimately elected. It has also been stated that the Act of Union received about as much respect for the "honour" of England on the world stage as did the Treaty of Limerick. Not many European countries cared for England at this particular time and the country was becoming more and more isolated on the world scene.

Over the next few years several attempts were made to again unite the Irishmen towards the cause of independence. Possibly among the most notable were the efforts of Robert Emmet, who united several factions of the United Irishmen and also again secured the promises of France to assist. A Rising was planned for 23 July 1803, and Emmet and his followers took to the Dublin streets. They encountered and killed the Lord Chief Justice of Ireland, Lord Kilwarden, but the French never showed up. It seems Napoleon Bonaparte was only using the Irish, their hopes, and his promises to them, as pawns in his much larger scheme. Robert Emmet's brother, Thomas Addis Emmet, declared that, "Bonaparte was the worst enemy Ireland ever had"(MacManus, 1990). Robert Emmet, along with seventeen of his followers, was publicly hung, and some accounts say beheaded, in front of Dublin Castle on the twentieth of December 1803.

Watching all this was a young solicitor (lawyer) by the name of Daniel O'Connell who had been born on the sixth of August 1775 in County Kerry. His uncle Daniel had been one of the "Wild Geese". In young Daniel's youth he had watched John Paul Jones chasing the British ships around the seas of Ireland. When the heavily oppressed Catholics of the early Nineteenth Century were being told that their best course of action was that of "dignified silence", the young O'Connell began urging the Irish towards agitation.

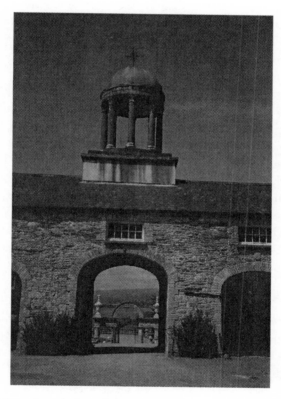

Looking through to the beautiful sea from the museum courtyard at Bantry Bay.

The Nineteenth Century

The Nineteenth Century began with the Act of Union taking effect on 1 January 1801, creating the United Kingdom of Great Britain and Ireland. This, along with Catholic Emancipation and Land Reform, became the major focal points regarding most of the political debate and activity for the majority of the century.

In the last lecture we discussed briefly the failed attempt by Robert Emmet and his followers to rise up on the night of the twenty-third of July 1803. Robert Emmet had been born at 124 St. Stephens Green, Dublin on the fourth of March 1778. He was expelled from Trinity College for his work with the United Irishmen. Emmet was an old-school revolutionary who wanted no part of this Act of Union. He had also served a short prison term for his work with the United Irishmen and when he was released went to Paris, met with Bonaparte and Talleyrand, and attempted to perfect his knowledge and skills regarding the implementation of a proper revolution. He then returned to Ireland and gathered as many of the like-minded former United Irishmen as he could and began military training in preparation for the rising.

His father had died and left him a few thousand pounds, all of which he spent on weapons, explosives, and ammunition. He had secretly established two munitions factories in Dublin, and when one accidentally exploded in early 1803, it placed the police and British administration on alert. Also, when he and his friend Thomas Russell tested an exploding rocket in the streets of Rathfarnham, the British again took notice. The rising was doomed from the very beginning, and as was mentioned, Emmet and seventeen of his followers were executed on the twentieth of September 1803 at Dublin Castle. Thomas Russell was betrayed and hung in County Down on the twenty-first of October 1803. This 1803 rising had little practical impact at the time, but provided a romantic and nationalistic sentiment that became deeply imbedded in the peoples' hearts and minds; and, provided great material for generations of balladeers. The final words of Robert Emmet, "Let no man write my epitaph; for as no man who knows my motives dare now vindicate them, let not prejudice or ignorance asperse them…When my country takes her place among the nations of the earth, then, at not till then, let my epitaph be written"; and, the words of such profound people as Jonathan Swift, Edmund Burke, William Molyneux, Henry Grattan, Theobald Wolfe Tone, and now Robert Emmet could not be erased, and were now held true and dear by the hopeful Irish Catholics. (All of the above were educated at Trinity College and I often wonder what Queen Elizabeth I would have thought about these developments from the university she founded in 1592, as something of an attempt to eliminate the Irish Catholic society.)

Discussed in the last section along with Robert Emmet and Thomas Emmet (who after serving a prison term for his activities with the United Irishmen from 1798 until 1802, moved to France, and then on to America in 1804) were such figures as Theobald Wolfe Tone and Napper Tandy. We watched the progression from the Irish Volunteers and Defenders to the United Irishmen, and then on to the development of the Catholic Committee. And on the other side we saw the rise of the Peep-o'-Day Boys and the Orange Society. An interesting phenomenon began to occur at this time that dramatically altered the course of Irish Nationalism. I earlier mentioned that the British began to employ a strategy of separating the Catholics from the Presbyterian dissenters through the use of exploiting the differences of their religious ideologies. Well this policy began to have rewards for the British as a wave of fervent fundamentalism swept through the Presbyterian community of northeastern Ireland. It is debatable however that it really had as much to do with religious conviction as it did with political and economic gain. This point has often been debated by the Irish historians and academics.

Hard-line Presbyterian orthodoxy under the leadership of the Reverend Henry Cooke triumphed over the more libertarian ideals, and became extremely inflexible. Cooke was born in County Derry in May of 1788, the son of a tenant farmer. He was educated in Glasgow and ordained a Presbyterian minister in 1808. Over the next sixty years Cooke would undertake a campaign to drive Arians, Unitarians, Catholics, and all who were not Presbyterians from Ulster. He organized a massive anti-Repeal rally when Daniel O'Connell visited Belfast in 1841. He secured British funding for Presbyterian schools and the Presbyterian College in Belfast, becoming its first president in 1847. The Act of Union had led to the trade embargoes with England being lifted and this Presbyterian segment of the population represented a fair portion of the Belfast businessmen. They began to see their ties with England as being very profitable and beneficial, and withdrew violently from joining the republicans in their nationalistic efforts. They began to see themselves in both religion and politics as something of the divine gatekeeper if you will. They somewhat began considering themselves as a higher more worthy form of citizen, and it is interesting to note how similar many of the attitudes of the Northern Ireland Unionists were to those towards blacks, and Irish, a bit later on in America.

Finally it was noted in the last lecture that a young solicitor by the name of Daniel O'Connell had been watching all this transpire. I believe we mentioned that Daniel O'Connell was born in County Kerry, on the sixth of August 1775, in Cahircaveen on Ireland's beautiful southwest coast.

His family had made a rather substantial fortune in the smuggling business. We discussed the very stringent and oppressive restrictions the English had placed on Irish imports and exports. The O'Connells imported a great many items that were either unavailable or prohibitively expensive if purchased from English merchants, such as continental foodstuffs, wine, European cloth; and, they lived in the near perfect location, on the sea, surrounded by mountain ranges that pretty much isolated them from the remainder of Ireland. Daniel's uncle, also named Daniel, was one of the "Wild Geese" and helped organize shipments from France, Spain, and Italy.

Daniel first broke onto the national scene in 1808, at the age of thirty-three years, when he became the spokesman for the more militant faction of the Catholic Committee, demanding equal rights for Catholics. The British Parliament had agreed to remove a few minor restrictions on Catholics and O'Connell claimed the action was not near the scope that it should be; and, also the legislation contained a clause that allowed the English to review all correspondence and interactions between Rome and the Irish Catholic Church. O'Connell went to Pope Pius VII himself and called for Catholic action and agitation. At that time the Catholic hierarchy in Ireland, represented by the "Catholic Board", had become quite demure and conciliatory, following years of terror and brutality. But, Ireland had now found a new leader and by 1811, the Catholic Board was so bold and militant that the English outlawed it. A few years later O'Connell began an association with the United Irishmen in Dublin and further developed his nationalist sentiments although many debate he should have taken his nationalistic ideals to yet another more militant level.

He was thrust into the position of National Hero basically as the result of two further incidents: one was the trial of John Magee in 1813, and the second was his duel with a retired English naval officer and Orangeman by the name of D'Esterre.

In 1813, the newspaper known as *The Evening Star*, which was owned by Magee, wrote the truth about the murder and oppression being perpetuated by such English agents as Westmoreland, Camden, and Cornwallis. The Government immediately brought charges against Magee and he employed O'Connell as his solicitor. The Government Attorney General, an avid Irish-hating Orangeman by the name of Saurin, decided to handle the prosecution himself. The entire jury was composed of Orangemen, as was the Lord Chief Justice.

O'Connell saw that his client had basically no chance whatsoever, so he lashed into a scathing attack of this mockery of justice; and, of the British system of Government. He taunted and scoffed at the Lord Chief Justice, the Prosecutor, and the jury calling them hypocrites and liars. This speech was considered his best of over hundreds that he would eventually deliver, and was published in its entirety the next day in Dublin, in a newspaper called *The Post*, along with various political cartoons—the most famous of which depicted Saurin as a beaten and profusely sweating pig.

His actions infuriated the English who actually tried to have him removed from the practice of Law. He simply ignored them and embraced the overwhelming gratitude of the Irish people; and, realized that mass political organization by Catholics was a necessity. He organized an alternative Irish parliament, comprised of prominent Catholic lawyers, and they began conducting meetings at O'Connell's headquarters in Dublin, which was located in the Corn Exchange Building on Burgh Quay. These in essence became political education classes for Catholics and others outside the ascendancy class. In 1826, this group under the sponsorship of the Catholic Association slated a candidate that defeated one from an old elite family, the Beresford's, in the Waterford Parliamentary election. Catholics won several other seats that year as well. Catholics were not allowed however sit in the English Parliament. Daniel O'Connell swore this would not be the case for long and in 1828 ran himself as the candidate from County Clare.

If anything could have possibly further endeared "The Counsellor", as he was now affectionately being called, to the hearts of the Irish people, it was certainly his duel with D'Esterre—an exceptional pistol shot who had been recruited by the Orangemen to challenge O'Connell.

In early 1815 D'Esterre sent word to O'Connell, while Daniel was arguing a case in the Four Courts that D'Esterre was planning to pummel him when he exited the building and would be waiting for him on Grafton Street. Well when O'Connell came out he grabbed a blackthorn walking stick and headed for Grafton Street. By the time he arrived at the appointed location, a crowd of thousands had gathered and D'Esterre hurriedly rolled up his horsewhip and snuck out the rear door of a beauty parlor.

D'Esterre next challenged O'Connell to a pistol duel, of which D'Esterre was considered an expert. They agreed on a secret location in County Kildare to escape the throngs, and were to be accompanied by only a few friends and a surgeon. Well, somehow the word leaked out and by the time they reached the appointed location, there was a substantial crowd already gathered. D'Esterre showed up half-an-hour late. The men faced off and at the drop of the handkerchief D'Esterre stepped to one side in an attempt to confuse O'Connell as both shots rang out. D'Esterre fell mortally wounded, and Daniel O'Connell was at this point in history, the undisputed leader of the Irish people.

O'Connell, as well as having incorporated nationalist sentiments, was still somewhat awed by the symbolism and spectacle of the English Royal throne; and, had in reality hoped that someday England and Ireland could live in harmony and peace—perhaps he was something of an idealist if you will. He had opposed the violent actions of 1798 and 1803, and at one point even proposed a "Royal Georgian Club", where the English and Irish could mingle and socialize at least six times per year, and march together wearing rosettes of royal blue, the combination of their green and orange. He even at one time, following the Irish visit of George IV in 1821, proposed the construction of an Irish royal residence, offering to contribute twenty pounds per year towards its maintenance.

George IV did in fact make some concessions, and perhaps held a dear spot in his heart for Ireland, as he spoke fondly of Ireland for some time after returning from that visit. O'Connell had the Irish people's mixed support for his policies of planned cooperation. In 1821, the English House of Commons passed the Catholic Relief Bill, which would have permitted Catholics to hold many government positions and would have made Catholics eligible for Parliament; but, it also contained one unacceptable clause—that being the Catholic Bishops must swear an oath of allegiance to the Royal Crown.

O'Connell had to basically start over. He found it a particularly good time for agitation, and also founded a new Catholic Association, organized by parishes. The churches and the priests then became the natural unifying points and leaders respectively. A dues or fee of one pence (penny) per month was charged of all members, and this was collected at the chapel's door on the first Sunday of each month. This became known as the "Catholic Rent", and soon gave the Catholic Association an income of over one-thousand pounds per week, and in a relatively short time the entire country was more organized, and possibly more unified, than it had ever been before. It must be noted here that perhaps the process and methods of winning emancipation were no less important than the actual gaining of emancipation itself.

The people were again watching world affairs and saw Simon Bolivar securing Independence for South America—Ireland even sent him a brigade to assist, led by Morgan O'Connell, Daniel's son. They also saw the Greeks gaining their Independence from the Turks. These events inspired, motivated, and emboldened the Irish populace to an attitude perceived as dangerous by the British government. They suppressed the Catholic Association, declaring it was not recognized in the eyes of the law.

In 1825, a compromise was penned, called the "Emancipation Bill". One provision of the bill was that the Catholic clergy was to be paid by the British government. This, the British hoped, would inspire the loyalty of both the clergy and the Irish people. The bill passed the House of Commons and would probably have passed the House of Lords, but the king's brother, the Duke of York, began an angry and threatening campaign outlining the evils of the bill. The bill was ultimately dismissed from the House of Lords, with the House of Lords itself being dissolved in an angry frenzy of confusion, and once again an anti-Catholic fervor arose in the country of England.

O'Connell had to start anew and founded the "New Catholic Association", to replace the outlawed "Catholic Association". It was organized "for the purpose of public and private charity and such other purposes as are not forbidden by the statute of George IV". By this simple name change and the changing of the statement of purposes to things that were not recently outlawed in the "Suppression

Act", O'Connell's movement never lost momentum. It in fact gained momentum, and solidarity, fed again by the extreme anti-Catholic sentiment now appearing to sweep through Britain.

In 1826, the results of the Parliamentary elections in Britain were overwhelmingly in favor of the conservative "anti-popery" movement. In Ireland, they were the exact opposite, overwhelmingly dominated by the Catholics. In 1828, a Parliamentary vacancy came up from the region of Clare. The people convinced Daniel O'Connell to run. (Remember, no Catholic was still permitted to hold a seat in Parliament.) This election, from all accounts was quite some spectacle. The ascendancy landowners were intimidating and threatening their tenants, and the priests were urging the people to vote from their hearts for the first time in their lives. Most everyone was in the streets with political signs, brass bands competed to be the loudest, and singing choruses harmonized their candidate's virtues. The election voting lasted for one week, six days actually, Monday through Saturday, and everyday tens of thousands were in the streets. In the end, O'Connell won by a margin of two-to-one. Sir Robert Peel at first declared that he could never consent to a Roman Catholic setting in the House of Commons; but, within a few months when he realized that five-sixths of Britain's military was trying to keep peace in Ireland, he declared, "I consider such a state of things much worse than rebellion".

In 1829, the "Emancipation Bill" was introduced to parliament. It narrowly passed over fierce opposition. Lord Wellington apologized for bringing it to the House of Lords, stating only that it was less evil than war. At first the king, George IV, refused to sign it, ranting and raving, and threatening just about everyone in any way associated. Peel and Wellington both resigned after being the subjects of substantial abuse, and the king was unable to find people willing to serve in a new ministry. He then recalled Peel and Wellington, signed the Bill in a rage, and throwing the pen upon the ground, stomped up and down on it screaming that he had "betrayed God and the English people". In theory, Catholics could now hold government positions and were entitled to the same rights as others; but, as we shall see, they would still suffer from the same previously developed prejudices for many generations, in parts of Ireland quite possibly yet up until this very day.

Following Emancipation, O'Connell's popularity grew even more renowned. He was now considered one of the greatest men in Europe, and certainly one of the greatest in Ireland's history. He then gave up his law practice and took up the causes of the people. This is when the famous "Tribute" was begun. It was a donation given by the people of Ireland for the support of Daniel O'Connell. It ranged from ten thousand to fifty thousand pounds per year, each of which was well earned by O'Connell and well spent by him for the people's causes, according to virtually all published reports of the time.

After Emancipation had been won (it was mentioned that the process was as important as the act itself, as it brought great confidence to the Irish people that they could themselves in fact affect change. It was also very symbolic in the fact that this marked the end of the penal system.), the next major step was to repeal the Act of Union. O'Connell started a weekly "repeal breakfast" and proclaimed that if these were suppressed by the British government, he would then initiate Repeal Lunches, Repeal Teas, Repeal Dinners, Repeal Suppers, and Repeal Feasts. He then began no less than eight organizations advocating repeal of the Act of Union, each of these taking the place of its outlawed predecessor. Among these were the General Association for Ireland, A Body of Persons, A Party Meeting for Dinner, the Repeal Association, the Irish Society for Legal and Legislative Relief, the Anti-Union Association, the Association of Irish Volunteers for Repeal of the Union, and the Association of Subscribers to the Parliamentary Intelligence Office. He so exhausted and infuriated the British government that they finally arrested him. He argued the court case himself, dragging it out for over a year, until the law charging him, the "Act for Suppression of Illegal Societies", had expired.

Molly Malone sells cockles and mussels outside Trinity College.

He then somewhat backed off from the repeal effort and led the fight for the removal of tithes. The protestant Church of England and its counterpart in Ireland, the Church of Ireland, were supported by mandatory tithes that all persons were forced to pay, amounting to one-tenth of their income. The Irish Catholics hated this law, as it made them pay for an extremely wealthy church that didn't even service one-tenth of the population, and none of them, while these same Irish people often didn't even have enough food to eat. In many of the more Catholic regions, often protestant ministers were receiving an enormous income and church fund for preaching to no one other than their own family.

Government employees, called process-servers, came around to collect the tithes. People began not paying, so the process-servers then employed and brought along armed guards, who would confiscate their cattle or whatever they could extract of value. In County Wexford during the summer of 1830, seventeen Irish farmers were killed by these "government workers", while the farmers were trying to take back their own cattle that had been seized. In November of that year, eighteen process-servers and guards were killed while trying to confiscate cattle in County Kilkenny. The "Tithe War" was escalating rapidly and becoming an ever more resented symbol of oppression. Twenty-five men were put on trial in County Kilkenny and Daniel O'Connell went to defend them. He destroyed the government's case against them and the men were set free. The Tithe War raged on with the government trying everything to accomplish the now impossible task of collecting this money. Finally, in 1838, the tithe was reduced by one-fourth and payment shifted to being the responsibility of the landlords. Most of them then attempted to raise the rents as their only recourse, but this didn't work as the farmers refused to pay—and the landlords either needed the workers; or, would evict the workers only to find that no one else would work for them.

Following the Tithe War, O'Connell again turned his attention toward repeal of the Act of Union. In 1841, there was elected for the first time in history a Nationalist Corporation to oversee the affairs of Dublin City, replacing the old Orangemen-dominated Dublin Corporation. To the joy of over five-sixths of Ireland, Daniel O'Connell was elected the first Nationalist Lord Mayor of Dublin. In his acceptance speech he stated that he would be fair and non-political in all dealings, but would be a "Repealer to my last breath". O'Connell had been very disappointed by the fact that the Reform Act of 1832 had not restored the forty-shilling freehold vote. (Following the great number of Catholic victories in the elections of 1826, the freehold vote had been raised to ten pounds and most Irish poor could never afford this amount.) By 1840, it was clear that the Whig-led government, under Lord Melbourne, that O'Connell had supported and actually helped put into power, was going to be defeated by the much more conservative and less sympathetic Tory government, led by Sir Robert Peel. "The Liberator", as Daniel O'Connell was now being called, became more aggressive and decided to more vigorously press for the repeal of the Act of Union.

In 1840, he formed the National Repeal Association, mentioned previously. He declared 1843 "Repeal Year" and forty "Monster Meetings" were then scheduled throughout the country. The London Times officially reported that a million people attended the meeting held on the Hill of Tara, legendary seat of the Irish High King, but other reports indicated there were far more, perhaps even twice that number. The National Repeal Association, and a deep passion for the repeal of the Act of Union, grew and O'Connell called for a general meeting of all Irish citizens to be held on 8 October 1843, at Clontarf, the place of Brian Boru's great victory over the Danes. Literally millions were expected to attend. The British government got nervous, and banned the meeting, sending in five regiments of soldiers with dozens of cannons and full artillery, and gunboats up the River Liffey. O'Connell, who really always believed in constitutional solutions, called for calm and gave way. He told his Repealers that, "nothing would justify his permitting vast masses of unarmed men to be mowed down".

The next morning, the government arrested O'Connell, his son John, several leaders of the movement, including two priests, and the editors of three nationalist papers, *The Freeman's Journal, The Pilot,* and *The Nation.* They were charged with "conspiring to change the constitution by illegal methods", and were tried by a court exclusively comprised of Orangemen. No Catholic was permitted to serve in any capacity. O'Connell was sentenced to one year in prison (being pardoned after three months by the House of Lords), given a two-thousand pound fine, and was given another seven years of probation during which time he could organize no political nor civic associations whatsoever. After he was released from jail, he was never quite the same and had lost much of the fire that had characterized his younger days. (As opposed to Samuel Beckett who claimed to gather fire with age and stated it was a good thing he didn't have such fire as a young man.)

During O'Connell's time in prison, the Repeal movement also lost much of its fire; and, in the following year, 1845, the first potato blight hit Ireland initiating the Great Famine, or more accurately now called the Great Hunger (*An Gorta Mor* in Irish), as these years saw substantial exports of Irish-grown crops by the wealthy ascendancy landlords. The Irish people were now starving and had far more on their minds than Repeal of the Act of Union. O'Connell died on 15 May 1847. Daniel O'Connell is a bit controversial in the fact many believe he should have taken a far more adversarial approach when dealing with England, as opposed to attempting to appease Britain and "backing down" at a couple of crucial junctures.

While O'Connell was in jail, a new movement was however taking shape that should be here mentioned for their continued later influence. As O'Connell may have been losing some of his fire this new group was kindling fires that would not be extinguished until they burned in the streets of Dublin during the Rising of 1916. It was formed by a group of journalists who became known as "Young Ireland". The three generally attributed with forming the organization, as well as the very influential nationalist newspaper called *The Nation,* were Thomas Davis, his close college friend and barrister, John Blake Dillon, and a journalist by the name of Charles Gavan Duffy. Another organizer was John Mitchel, who was much more the revolutionary, believed in armed rebellion and established a journal called the *United Irishman;* and, I've been told was also an ancestor of the American Legislator, George Mitchell, who helped negotiate the 1998 "Belfast Agreement".

These Young Irelanders kept the fight alive, but as was previously mentioned the Great Hunger ultimately prohibited the people from having much time for organization and unification. Thomas Davis, probably the most prolific and influential of the writers, died from a mysterious disease in 1845, as the others were preparing for their armed rebellion that became known as the Rising of 1848. Mitchel and most of the leaders were arrested in 1848, after the Young Irelanders had moved from literary agitation to armed rebellion, initiating a skirmish at Ballingarry in County Tipperary, under the questionable military competence of one William Smith O'Brien.

Some of the leaders fled to America and many were shipped to the Australian island of Tasmania (Van Diemen's Land). John Mitchel escaped from the British jail in Australia and went to America, where he published his most influential work the *Jail Journal.* This was a brilliantly written story of an apocalyptic struggle of one nation's eight hundred year fight against an extremely sadistic oppressor who attempted to dehumanize then eradicate the people of this nation. The oppressor's final act was a premeditated attempt to depopulate the nation through an artificially sustained famine. Following the publication of this work, many have said that Nationalism virtually became a secular religion in Ireland.

The Great Hunger began with a potato blight first seen in 1845 and lasted into the winter of 1849-1850. Many scholars believe this is the great dividing line in Irish history. In 1845, Ireland's population was over eight million, having grown rapidly from around five million at the time of the Act of Union (1801); but, by 1850, over one million had died, and another two and a half million refugees had emigrated, and people were still leaving at the rate of a quarter of a million per year. Before the famine, Irish was the predominant language in Ireland, but following the famine English was spoken almost everywhere except along parts of the western coastal areas, now known as Gaeltacht areas.

The long-term effects of the Great Famine were immense, and in some respects are felt to this very day. The upward social mobility of the population was halted, the traditional hostility between tenants and landlords was magnified as many landlords were seen as having ignored the plight of the people, and a greater hostility or resentment towards the British government developed as they were seen as taking inadequate measures to relieve the suffering. An enduring bitterness developed among the Irish people who could not escape the visions of people starving to death while livestock and grain were being exported from Ireland, often under military guard. Poverty was the only disease, and poverty is never a natural disaster, but the byproduct of a greater wealth accumulated by a few.

The extremely moving Famine sculpture outside the Harp Tavern in Sligo town.

The ruins of a home abandoned during the famine years, with Ben Bulben in the background

The potato was the staple food of the impoverished Irish people, as more calories per acre can come from raising potatoes than any other crop. Over 130,000 families were attempting to survive on one acre of land or less (Gallagher, 1995), and when there was total crop failure of the potato in 1846, the affects were devastating. Most of these families were before the blight barely surviving, living in one-room mud cabins without windows, and sharing these cabins with an average of ten other people (Gallagher, 1995). The British called them paupers and claimed the hunger and blight were their own fault. An undersecretary to the British Treasury, Charles Trevelyan, the man given the responsibility for Irish famine relief, stated publicly on several occasions that he believed the famine was divine retribution.

The British government supposedly claimed they were only following the prevailing economic philosophy at the time, known as the Manchester School Doctrine, which believed the state should never interfere in the natural workings of economic laws. One text asked, quite astutely I thought, whether the British would have been near as dedicated to the Manchester School Doctrine if the famine had been centered in say, Manchester. It must always be remembered that the famine in Ireland posed no threat to the English, and was most likely seen by most of the British as actually helping to alleviate a long-standing threat or problem; hence, there is possibly nothing mysterious about England's lack of urgency to assist the Irish people.

Mass evictions of their Irish tenants by British landlords were highly encouraged by the British Prime Minister, Lord Russell, and others such as Lord Palmerstown whose agents "emigrated" over two thousand people from his Sligo lands in 1847 alone, as these lands could then be better used for the grazing of livestock. Many landlords even paid their tenants' emigration fares to America and elsewhere. In March of 1846, the entire village of Ballinglass was evicted so the land could be used for grazing.

The ideals of the "Young Ireland" movement had been preserved forever in the hearts and minds of these famine refugees. Some had settled in France and were inspired by the passionate revolutionary ideals permeating that society. Others had gone to America and joined forces with the large Irish populations of the eastern coast, especially New York, Boston and Philadelphia—mostly people who had fled the famine. A fellow named James Stephens (who the British believed was dead after a mock funeral was held in Kilkenny in 1848) organized these American refugees into what would become the very influential resource base for Irish nationalism, the Fenian Brotherhood, and then covertly returned to Ireland and on St. Patrick's Day, 1858, officially founded the "secret" society there known as the "Fenian Brotherhood" (Fenian being derived from Finn McCool's legendary band of warriors called the "fianna"). It was soon to become known in Ireland as the "Irish Republican Brotherhood", and this name was officially adopted after a reorganization of the Republican movement in 1873. Stephens was a devoted follower of Theobald Wolfe Tone and spent his entire lifetime in pursuit of obtaining WolfeTone's objectives.

The Fenian Brotherhood was also formalized in America on St. Patrick's Day, 1858, and those in exile there were to tap America's vast resources to assist with funds, manpower, and weaponry. The Fenians now saw no hope outside of armed revolution, and for this were denounced by the Catholic Church. Stephens then began publishing a newspaper called *The Irish People* in 1863, and used the American Civil War as an example and training ground for the study of maneuvers, intelligence, strategy, and tactics. The membership oath for these two organizations was drafted, or more accurately revised, by Thomas Clarke Luby and was really quite simple and would remain the same for several generations, "I _____ _____, in the presence of the Almighty God, do solemnly swear allegiance to the Irish Republic, now virtually established, and that I will do my very utmost at every risk, while life lasts, to defend its independence and integrity; and, finally, that I will yield implicit obedience in all things, not contrary to the laws of God, to the commands of my superior officers. So help me God, Amen."(Kenny, 1994)

Stephens was arrested in November of 1865, along with several other Fenian leaders and locked under maximum security in Richmond Jail, Dublin. One morning he was mysteriously gone, his jail cell standing wide open. It was later learned that his jailer was also a Fenian. This made sensational headlines throughout Europe. The British were infuriated and for almost three weeks continuously searched every corner of Dublin to no avail. All of a sudden one day a magnificent carriage and four horses pulled up to a house in Dublin, Stephens got in and paraded through the streets of Dublin before boarding a ship bound for France. All the coachmen were well armed Fenians, and before a large enough police force could be summoned, Stephens was on a ship and sailing for France. A few months later he was back in America.

The Fenians of Ireland by 1865 numbered over 100,000. Fenians were also active among the Irish population in England, and in September of 1867, they attempted to seize Chester Castle, a large arms depot. They were unsuccessful and five Fenians were captured. Three of these were executed (William Allen, Michael Larkin, and Michael O'Brien) following an escape attempt where a British guard was killed. The other two Fenians involved, Thomas Kelly and John McCafferty, successfully escaped. These executions only added fuel to the raging Fenian fire. The three executed became known as the "Manchester Martyrs".

History indicates that the Fenians were perhaps strongest, and most efficiently organized in America. They were even sold quantities of arms by the American government on several occasions, and originally were encouraged and permitted to meet freely in America. (Remember, most in America had no love for the British either.)

One of the Fenian plans devised among the American group even called for the invasion of Canada. Historical records indicate that this action was known about in advance by the American government (this fact placed great strain on British-American relations for several years); and, was in fact initiated on 31 May 1866. The invasion was to be a three-pronged assault, launched from Vermont in the east, Buffalo in the central regions, and Chicago in the west. The Buffalo-based group was the only one really getting off the ground; and, General John O'Neill led a band of Fenians that captured the British Fort Erie. They next drove back a Canadian army regiment at a place called Limestone Ridge on 2 June 1866. Public opinion then forced America to declare that they could not condone this, and no more Fenians would be permitted to cross the border; but those already there were allowed to return to America safely. O'Neill actually tried invading Canada on two more occasions, in 1870 and 1871, briefly capturing the Canadian town of Pembina, Manitoba, in 1871. This was basically the end of the Fenian movement in the United States, as it was being rapidly replaced by the "Clan na Gael" (the Irish Race), which would develop into the most enduring and effective of the American republican movements.

Except for a couple of rather insignificant Irish risings in 1865 and 1867, and the invasion of Canada, the Fenian movement didn't accomplish a great deal from a military standpoint, but it was extremely influential in perpetuation of the revolutionary mentality, and it brought a number of more accomplished political minds to the forefront. From out of the Fenian movement came a uniquely creative political concept, the combining of revolutionary conspiracy with open agrarian agitation and parliamentary action. This new movement was termed the "New Departure" and was organized by John Devoy in America, and Michael Davitt in Ireland. (Both men had served prison terms for their participation in the Fenian movement.)

In the 1869 Act, the official Established Church of England, which had previously been forced upon the people, was disestablished. In the following year, the first land act, The Land Act of 1870, was made law. It gave the right of compensation to all evicted tenants for any expenses they had made towards improvements to their properties. These don't seem like much today, and it is true they were even inadequate at the time, but they were very symbolic in the fact that they marked the beginning of an end to the ascendancy landlord class in Ireland. British Prime Minister Gladstone was a former associate of Robert Peel, now heading up the liberal government, and he took great abuse from the English, and later stated that the actions of the Fenians had forced him to initiate both these measures.

Two issues pretty much dominated the 1870's and 1880's. These were namely "Home Rule" and "Land Reform"; and, they were generally interrelated. One of the best solicitors in Dublin was a Tory Member of Parliament for Trinity College by the name of Isaac Butt. He was retained to defend the Fenian prisoners in Dublin. He came to learn a great deal about the Fenian ideals; and, ironically became a major advocate for the cause of Irish Independence. He invented a new term, "Home Rule". A "Home Government Association" was formed (it was later renamed the "Home Rule League"). Its first meeting was held in a Dublin Hotel in 1870, and it passed a resolution stating, "The true remedy for the evils of Ireland is the establishment of an Irish Parliament with full control over our domestic affairs". The old demand for the repeal of the Act of Union was discarded, and the new demand was for "Home Rule", which by its very nature implied a much broader scope.

The next step involved organizing a new political party, but Butt was not really effective in leading this new party. His vision was slightly different than that of most Irishmen. He envisioned a federal system in which Ireland would also continue to send delegates to the English Parliament at Westminster. The man who sculpted the new party advocating first Land Reform and then Home Rule, from then on called the Irish Parliamentary Party, was a southern Irish protestant by the name of Charles Stewart Parnell. He was an Irish landlord, elected to parliament from County Meath in 1875. His great-grandfather, Sir John Parnell was one of the "Incorruptibles" who voted against the Act of Union in 1800. His mother was an American whose father, Commodore Charles Stewart, had fought in the War of 1812 against the British. The family had emigrated to America from Belfast just prior to the American Revolution, along with many other Ulster-Irish, commonly called Scots-Irish, that at the time were also being persecuted by the British, so needless to say the family had no great love for England.

Parnell was not a great orator, but he was an efficient organizer, basing his actions on sound political judgments; and, he also possessed a rather commanding personal charisma. In 1877, Isaac Butt died and after the elections of 1880, Parnell took over sole leadership of the party. He was also President of the Irish National Land League, which had been created in October 1879.

The Land League was actually the brainchild of Michael Davitt, who had served over seven years in Dartmoor prison for his part in the Fenian raid on Chester Castle. Davitt had lost his right arm in a Lancashire textile mill at the age of eleven with no compensation, and his family had been evicted from their family land during the famine, so he most avidly wished to pursue the Fenian ideals. (Michael Davitt's father organized one of the very first secret agrarian societies in County Mayo.) The Land League sought what they called the "Three F's"—fair rent, fixed tenure, and the free sale of tenancy at a fair market value.

Between 1870 and 1876, there were fourteen legislative efforts to amend the Land Laws, all being unsuccessful. The landlords were asking rents that the land could not produce, and in 1876-1878, there were again crop failures that bordered on famine. A couple of the more abusive landlords were shot, including one named Lord Leitrim in Donegal, who supposedly asked exorbitant rents and then often demanded the tenants' wives and daughters be given as payment. He also employed armed enforcers and after the most violent of these was found dead he evicted all tenants from his land.

The Land League developed a new strategy, if a landlord (or his agent) was charging exorbitant rents, was abusive, or unfairly evicted a tenant, the League would concentrate public opinion on these estates by holding mass meetings to ostracize the individual. They would then refuse to provide any services to the landlord, generally making life as difficult as possible; and, then would not allow anyone else to occupy the land where a tenant was unfairly evicted, nor do any business with that particular landlord.

The most famous example of these practices occurred in 1880, when the Land League directed their attention towards an English Captain named Charles Boycott, whose name has forever since been incorporated into our language. Boycott was famous for evicting tenants and keeping their money and property, and eventually he could not get his crops harvested from the fields, nor could he get his horses shod, nor his carriages repaired. He asked for British assistance. Eventually, fifty Orangemen from the north and a few hundred British soldiers came to assist him. They had to walk fifteen miles in the rain from the train station and then camped in his front yard. They had brought no provisions, because they reckoned if they were going to do his work, the Captain would supply their needs. They ate up all his cattle, pigs, turkeys, geese, chickens, and crops before leaving. Captain Boycott was far worse off after they had left, than before they had arrived.

Most all historians believe that the actions of the Land League were most probably so successful mainly through the substantial financial support from

America. It was also an extremely well organized effort and could have never been so effective without receiving the overwhelming popular support of the people as well. The movement envisioned that the political aspects would begin with the withdrawal from the English Parliament of all those supporting the Land League ideals. This strategy of succession would also be employed in the next century by the Sinn Fein party with a powerful and dramatic effect.

The "Gladstone Land Act of 1881", finally guaranteed the "Three F's", over violent opposition in the House of Lords. It was something of a catch-22, however because if the tenants made any improvements whatsoever to their homes, then their rents could be raised (Landlords never made any improvements nor repairs). In October 1881, Parnell was arrested under the Coercion Act and imprisoned in Dublin's Kilmainham Jail. When he was asked who would take his place, he remarked, "Captain Moonlight" (Groups of tenants who by night harassed abusive landlords were known as "Moonlighters"). Kilmainham jail was probably the most advantageous place for an Irish politician to be at this particular time, and the British government eventually realized that it better served their interests to have Parnell out of jail than in, and released him in May of 1882.

The "Irish National League" was formed in 1882, and placed its emphasis on Home Rule, rather than Land Reform. Parnell would have originally been content to accept for Ireland a subservient parliament, dealing exclusively with domestic affairs. In the election of 1885, however, Parnell's Irish Parliamentary Party won eighty-six seats in Parliament and held the balance of power between the Liberals, led by Gladstone, and the Conservatives, led by Lord Salisbury. Gladstone became Prime Minister with Parnell's support, and in April 1886, introduced his first "Home Rule Bill", which provided for both an Irish Parliament and an Irish Executive Branch. With ninety-three of Gladstone's Liberals voting against the bill it was defeated by a count of 343 votes to 313 votes. The Tory Conservatives then overwhelmingly won the next general election, with Parnell and Ireland already having been committed to the Liberal side.

In December 1889, Parnell was named as a co-respondent in a divorce action brought by an Irish Member of Parliament, Captain William O'Shea. Parnell offered no defense, and after the divorce he in fact married Kitty O'Shea. This cost him the leadership of his party and he died on 6 October 1891, at forty-five years of age, worn out, somewhat socially disgraced, and embittered. The Fenians supported Parnell and just before his death he had summoned James Stephens back to Ireland, who arrived just in time to place a wreath on Parnell's grave. It was Stephens and the ex-Fenians who carried on for Parnell and became very popular with the young, and not his ex-parliamentary associates. Parnell's most bitter rival, Tim Healy, once wrote, "We may have the Irish voters, but Parnell has their sons", and these were handed over to James Stephens. W. B. Yeats told the Swedish Academy in 1923, while receiving his Nobel Prize, that this was the "Fourth Bell", and that "The modern literature of Ireland, and indeed all that stir of thought which prepared for the Anglo-Irish War, began when Parnell fell from power in 1891".

The Irish Parliamentary Party and its leadership floundered for several years, and when John Redmond announced in the British House of Commons in 1914, that Irish soldiers would fight for England in World War I, after Ireland had already declared neutrality, the party disappeared from existence forever in something of a final disgrace.

Poet Willie Joe Meally reads at the Mackeral Festival's Literary Night.

The Gaelic League, Sinn Fein, and the Easter Rising

The revolutionary doctrine of the Fenians, originally derived from the beliefs of Wolfe Tone, reached vast numbers of the young Irish following the fall of Parnell, whom these young had practically been taught to worship. (One might say also that this era displayed the origins of a clerical backlash that may still be seen yet to this day in certain segments of the population. These young believed that the church had betrayed Parnell by denouncing him.) In 1893 The Gaelic League was formed by Dr. Douglas Hyde and Eoin MacNeill. This came on the heels of the Gaelic Athletic Association, which had been organized only a few years earlier in 1884, and was having great success in renewing pride and interest in traditional Irish athletics, such as hurling, Gaelic football, etc. Its primary founder was a very interesting fellow by the name of Major John MacBride, born in 1865 in Westport, County Mayo. He joined the Irish Republican Brotherhood in the 1880's, fought in the Boer War (1889-1902 South African War between the Dutch settlers and the British) against the English, married the beautiful actress, and republican activist and organizer, Maud Gonne in 1903, fought in the G.P.O. in 1916, and was executed by the English on 5 May of that year. The Gaelic League promoted the cultural aspects of traditional Ireland, especially the Irish language, art, literature, music, and drama.

Dr. Douglas Hyde was a very interesting and influential figure in the development of Irish nationalism and Irish pride. He was born in Castlerea, County Roscommon, in 1860. He had learned the Irish language and folk stories as a child from people in this very Irish region, and wrote poems in Irish as a youngster. He had a distinguished career at Trinity College, Dublin, and became a Doctor of Laws in 1888.

In 1892 he became president of the National Literary Society. Following a speech in which he called for Ireland to become de-Anglicized, he was invited to a nationalist meeting from which the Gaelic League was organized. He wrote several plays for the Abbey Theatre. He became a professor of Modern Irish at University College, Dublin in 1909 and held that position until 1932. Dr. Hyde became a senator in the Irish Free State in 1925-26 and then again in 1937. He was a highly regarded political figure that he was chosen as the first President of Ireland in 1938, under the new constitution. He held this position until the expiration of his term in 1945. He died in Dublin on 12 July 1949. His publication *A Literary History of Ireland,* from 1899 is still considered a monumental and most definitive work.

The writings and plays of William Butler Yeats, Lady Augusta Gregory, Standish O'Grady, John Millington Synge, Dr. Douglas Hyde, and increasing numbers of other writers and scholars led to an incredible revival of Irish pride, identity, and nationalistic sentiment. The National Literary Society, and the National Literary Theatre, were both founded by W. B. Yeats and Lady Gregory in 1899. These glorified and romanticized nationalistic ideals in such plays as *Cathleen ni Houlihan,* written by Yeats and starring the incredibly beautiful actress Maud Gonne. It was produced in 1902 and became immensely famous and almost worshipped among the young nationalists, as Cathleen symbolized Ireland's struggle for freedom and independence. The overall influence of the Gaelic League grew dramatically at this time throughout most segments of the population.

In 1899, Arthur Griffith began publication of a magazine called the *United Irishman,* whose contributors included some of the most accomplished minds of the day—in the fields of drama, essay writing, political prose, and current research. In 1903, the Abbey Theatre was founded, or perhaps better described as evolving from the Irish Literary Theatre, by William Butler Yeats and Lady Gregory, primarily to call further attention to nationalistic ideals. This yet drew more of the most accomplished playwrights of the day, with a strong emphasis on Irish heritage and nationalism. It opened with Yeats' play *On Baile's Strand* and Lady Gregory's play *Spreading the News,* and the Abbey Theatre has been immensely popular ever since, winning numerous awards, and always producing the most interesting and relevant of plays. Upon his death bed Yeats expressed concern that his plays led directly to the Rising of 1916 and the deaths of so many people.

A fervent nationalistic pride in all things "Irish" was rapidly developing. It is interesting to note that after centuries of serious attempts to unify the Irish people, it was finally coming about in the middle of the nineteenth century, primarily through the efforts of a variety of artistic and scholarly pursuits. Many scholars, including Professor Etienne Rynne of University College, Galway, have argued that a series of archaeological discoveries and the ensuing pride in these Irish antiquities, namely the Cross of Cong, The Tara Brooch, and the Ardagh Chalice (all found and presented to the Royal Irish Academy shortly before the formation of the Gaelic League), along with the great illuminated works such as The Book of Kells, The Book of Durrow, The Book of Armagh; and, the artistic, literary, and theatrical endeavors previously mentioned were the dominating factors in the fosterage of Irish Nationalism. It can be further argued that this fact still holds true today.

In 1905, Arthur Griffith and his friends brought to Ireland a new political movement based on a national identity, and immediately calling for withdrawal of Ireland's representatives from Westminster, and the establishment of an Irish Parliament with complete control over the affairs of Ireland.

Mr. Griffith began publication of a new weekly newspaper, which in effect replaced the *United Irishman* and was more politically orientated. It was called *Sinn Fein* (Irish—meaning "ourselves alone"). In *Sinn Fein*, Arthur Griffith showed Ireland how she could proceed in the handling all of her own affairs, including everything from establishing international commerce, to the establishment of rail and highway systems, to the coinage and printing of all her own money (the monetary unit was to be called the "gael"). Shortly after the publication of the weekly, Sinn Fein became a strong nationalistic political movement, and then an official political party, that helped lead the fight for Irish Independence. New feelings of Irish pride, potential, and accomplishment were evident everywhere, and the electricity in the air told everyone that the time was now right to strike for independence.

The Wyndham Act of 1903 finally permitted Irish Catholic tenants to buy and own their farms. A purchase price was calculated, and then paid, by the government to the landlords. The Irish tenant would then pay an annual annuity to the state.

A national mercantile marine was established to engage in commerce with the European continent, whose markets were much more lucrative for the Irish than were the English markets. For years the English merchants had been buying Irish products for unnaturally low prices, then immediately carrying them to the continent for resale, reaping huge profits in the process. Also a program of boycotting certain foreign products, to thus protect Irish industries, was put into practice as well. They even attempted to boycott Queen Victoria's visit to Dublin Castle in 1900. Arthur Griffith was a determined Nationalist and he refused to settle for anything falling short of that ultimate goal. He taught that nationalistic ideals were to be incorporated into every aspect of Irish life. And this began happening—in art, literature, drama, economics, industrial and social programs—at least in the southern two-thirds of Ireland.

In Ulster, the population was heavily Protestant, especially in the industrialized cities of the northeast, and they saw "Home Rule" as basically "Rome Rule", and many of them were still terrified by the proposition of a Catholic controlled society. They were led by a Dublin-born Tory lawyer by the name of Edward Carson, who was passionately determined to see Home Rule defeated. This group began threatening Civil War in Ireland and organized the Ulster Volunteer Force in 1912-1913. Many of their leaders were retired British army officers and they began pressing Britain for support. King George at first refused but was then told several current British military officers would resign if support was not rendered. In April of 1914, the first of several large shipments of arms and ammunition landed at Larne in County Antrim and were dispersed among the Ulster Volunteer Force. Following these developments, the Irish party now led by John Redmond reluctantly amended the Home Rule Bill, and permitted the Ulster counties to opt out if they so desired. This was initially to be for six years only, but as we all know, it has lasted until the time of this publication.

Arthur Griffith was also a patient man, carefully planning his strategy, while waiting for the perfect parliamentary moment, something similar to what Daniel O'Connell had tried to do. The highly emotional centenary celebrations of the 1798 Rebellion and the British problems associated with the outbreak of the Boer War had both boosted Irish morale and the belief that the perfect moment was very near. It came with the beginning of World War I.

Poet Willie Joe Meally, Kilkenny County Councilor John Brennan, and physician Andre Merrill inspect a beautiful new park developed from the ancient mines in Castlecomer, County Kilkenny.

At this time Sinn Fein, and a second Nationalistic movement called the Physical Force Party (actually a revived Irish Republican Brotherhood through the energetic efforts of Thomas Clarke, who had just returned from exile in America) began sharing ideas. The Physical Force Party published a magazine called "Irish Freedom", which also printed the works of several of the outstanding thinkers of the day, among them one of the most remarkable was Padraig Pearse, a teacher, poet and prose writer with strong nationalistic sentiments. The Physical Force Party also quite effectively influenced public opinion through a series of gatherings known as the "Wolfe Tone Clubs". Fenianism and Republicanism again became the key words, and the Fenians adopted a motto written by Fintan Lalor, "Repeal not the Union, but the conquest". Sinn Fein somewhat took a back seat to the more forceful Physical Force Party, who strongly believed the time was now right for Ireland to strike for independence when, in August of 1914, England became occupied with World War I. (Many historians also believe that the outbreak of World War I may have averted a civil war in Ireland between Unionists and Nationalists.)

Weapons began to be secured from the continent, especially from Germany, by smugglers who supplied the Irish Volunteers. The Irish Volunteers were at this time marching every Sunday on maneuvers, and on one occasion, 26 July 1914, the Irish Volunteers marched from Dublin out to the coastal city of Howth and blatantly met a ship loaded with arms in broad daylight and unloaded it. The Volunteers then marched back to Dublin before dispersing, each with his new weapon and a quantity of ammunition.

British soldiers had been assembled and marched to the outskirts of Dublin to find no one. On their way back to their barracks, the people began hooting and hollering at them and they fired two volleys into the crowd, killing four innocent people, and wounding approximately fifty more. All of Ireland was in shock, as was the rest of Europe. The funerals were massive affairs, with hundreds of thousands attending. The Volunteers protected the crowd, presented the Tricolour, and fired a military salute over the graves. This became tradition from then on at all Republican funerals. Everyone knew revolution was imminent and drawing near.

Gowran Castle gate and keep, a place where many secret meetings were held.

Next, England wanted Ireland to send the Volunteers to fight for England as her involvement in the war deepened. Both the political leaders and the Volunteers rejected the offer, and chose instead to parade through College Green and around the Parliament Building, on St. Patrick's Day of 1915, flying the Irish Tricolour.

Two extremely strong and dynamic personalities then came to the forefront as insurrection became eminent. These were the aforementioned Padraig Pearse, whose powerful and passionate philosophically orientated writings presented the Irish cause in a near spiritual context; and, James Connolly, a socialist who founded the Irish Socialist Republican Party and believed in the Marxist doctrine of Social Revolution. In 1913, Connolly organized a series of strikes by the Irish workers and organized the Irish Citizen Army to protect the workers from the police. (Sean O'Casey wrote his famous play *Red Roses for Me* about these strikes.) Both Pearse and Connolly believed that the English system of capitalistic commercialism was the most wicked and corrupt force that could be inflicted upon any nation, and saw it as the root cause of Ireland's problems. Both of these men were embraced deeply by the Irish Republican Brotherhood.

Connolly was the most determined, telling several friends as early as 1914 that he would not let the "great war" end without striking a blow for Irish freedom, and he stirred like sentiments throughout the country with the writings in his newspaper. During the period of Lent preceding the Easter Rising, he wrote such passionate, treasonous, and revolutionary material that a citizen armed guard stood watch day and night over his printing presses at Liberty Hall, anticipating the government to raid the premises at any moment, and this action, most believed would initiate the great rebellion. A week before Easter, the Irish Tricolour was raised over Liberty Hall as if the Republic had already been declared and established.

The Supreme Council of the Irish Republican Brotherhood voted almost unanimously (there was one dissenting vote) in January 1916 that a full-blown insurrection should be initiated "in the near future". The Executive Council of the Irish Volunteers was, but for a few exceptions, also composed of members of the I.R.B., and the I.R.B. men were instructed to take their orders from no one except Padraic Pearse, Thomas MacDonagh, or their delegates. The President of the Irish Volunteers was Professor Eoin MacNeill who was not a member of the I.R.B., and several records indicate that there was developing at this time considerable friction within the Irish Volunteers, between members who were I.R.B. men, and those who were not.

Padraic Pearse, who had been delegated the responsibility of mobilizing the insurrection, issued an order calling for the Rising to be held on Easter Sunday, 23 April 1916, without ever informing Eoin MacNeill. He also issued these orders in the provinces, not through the ranking Irish Volunteer officers, but through perhaps junior officers that were members of the I.R.B. MacNeill learned of the orders on Wednesday 19 April, and immediately issued a command counteracting the orders of Pearse, who did not learn of MacNeill's actions until late in the evening of Thursday 20 April. On Friday, Pearse, MacDonagh and Sean MacDermott went to visit Eoin MacNeill and clarified the situation for him. He promptly resigned and handed control of the Irish Volunteers over to the Irish Republican Brotherhood's Military Committee, but was not at all happy. Later on that day he reassumed command of the Irish Volunteers and again issued orders canceling all maneuvers. This was not learned about by the I.R.B. until late Saturday evening when Eoin MacNeill actually placed an advertisement in the newspaper. When the I.R.B. members and Military Council met early Easter Sunday, one could easily understand the confusion and agitation present.

A national organized insurrection was to be led by the Irish Volunteers (actually fronting for the I.R.B.) and, as was mentioned previously, scheduled for Easter Sunday. It was to develop from the ordinary marching and parade maneuvers into armed rebellion. However, also on Friday of the week preceding, Roger Casement and a German ship named the "Aud", disguised as a Norwegian timber ship, was intercepted by the British carrying over twenty-thousand rifles, millions of rounds of ammunition, machine guns, artillery, and explosives that were to supply the I.R.B./Volunteers. The German crew was forced to scuttle the ship. This was another reason that the panic stricken Eoin MacNeill, on again—off again chairman of the Volunteers, actually put an article in the newspapers on Saturday informing all Volunteers that, "Owing to the very critical position, all orders given to Irish Volunteers for tomorrow, Easter Sunday, are hereby rescinded, and no parades, marches, or other movements of Irish Volunteers will take place. Each individual Volunteer will obey this order strictly in every particular". (Macmanus, 1990)

Through the sinking of the Aud, the British learned of the planned insurrection and closed all telegraph offices on Easter Sunday, thus making accurate and efficient communication among the insurgents extremely difficult. The I.R.B. members who had gathered at Liberty Hall disbursed and went home, only to learn later that Pearse again ordered the Rising to proceed the following morning, Monday 24 April. Many received this message and many did not; and, those that did weren't at all certain which set of orders should be followed.

To a startled nation, shortly after noon on Monday, 24 April 1916, the Irish Tricolour was raised above the General Post Office in Dublin and the Irish Republic was proclaimed. It seems the British had planned to arrest all the Irish political leaders and leaders of the Volunteers within the following week. No sooner had this decision been made by the British, than it was relayed to the Irish through secret informers. The non I.R.B. members of the Volunteer Council also met on Easter Sunday and decided that it was basically "now or never", and voted to join the limited insurrection, now pretty much doomed to failure, the following day. The insurgents may have indeed doubted the likelihood of their success, but they were confident that this blow, and likely loss of Irish blood, would be the determining factor in the gaining of Irish Independence; and, they were correct.

The men fought bravely and there is little doubt that if the Aud had not gone down, the Irish would have most likely won on the field of battle. On Monday, 24 April, 1916, the Dublin Volunteers, sporting their weapons and one day's food rations occupied the General Post Office, the Four Courts, Liberty Hall, St. Stephen's Green, three train terminals, and several other minor locations surrounding the center of Dublin. They made two critical errors however—they did not attempt to occupy Trinity College nor Dublin Castle. Trinity College was an ideal fortress with its massive walls and city-within-a-city resources. It also held a commanding position of the Parliament Building and the two main Dublin thoroughfares. The Volunteers thought there were large numbers of troops inside, but this was not the case. They also thought Dublin Castle was protected by far more British troops than was actually the case. If the Volunteers had captured these two strategic locations, the British would have been forced to back down.

Anyway, the Proclamation of the Irish Republic was published on thousands of leaflets and several giant placards. There was actually very little fighting on Monday, mostly just sporadic sniper fire. The British were totally unprepared, thinking the Irish had abandoned the project, and could not gather their soldiers quickly enough, as the Irish forces dug in and fortified their positions.

On Tuesday, a force of approximately 4500 British troops finally secured the Castle and began attacking the Irish strongholds. By Wednesday, Liberty Hall had been mostly destroyed and by Thursday, much of O'Connell Street (at that time Sackville Street) was ablaze. The British forces then concentrated on destroying the rebels' headquarters, the General Post Office, over which the Republican Tricolour was still flying.

On Friday, an all-out bombardment had set basically the entire center of Dublin city ablaze. The numbers of non-combatant casualties were massive and still rising. On Saturday, the General Post Office was set aflame, and the Republican insurgents had to flee out the back to a new location on Moore Street. At noon Pearse sent a message, by way of a Red Cross Nurse, asking for terms. These were refused and at two o'clock in the afternoon, Pearse and the others surrendered unconditionally to the British commander, Sir John Maxwell.

Pearse then sent out word to the other Irish Commandants—Edward Daly at the Four Courts, Countess Markievicz, who had been driven from her position at Stephen's Green back to the College of Surgeons, Commandant Thomas McDonagh at Jacob's factory, Eamon deValera at Boland's Mills (they had prevailed and held the entire southern part of the city), and Commandant Eamonn Ceannt at the South Dublin Union, that they were told to lay down their arms. MacDonagh at first refused to obey this command, but did so the following day. For several nights snipers continued to fire upon the British troops who became increasingly angered.

A massive roundup of Irish Nationalists was then begun in all parts of the country. Many were sent to England and held in extremely unsanitary, rat-infested internment camps. Secret military trials were held and executions began. All of those signing the Republican Proclamation, and fifteen in all, were shot before world outrage forced the British to discontinue the executions, of which ninety had been scheduled. Those shot were Padraig and William Pearse, James Connolly, Eamonn Ceannt, Michael O'Hanrahan, Sean MacDermott, Con Colbert, J.J. Heuston, Thomas Ceannt (who was shot in County Cork), Joseph Mary Plunkett, Edward Daly, Michael Mallon, Thomas MacDonagh, Thomas Clarke, and John MacBride. The great majority of the remainder of those sentenced received amnesty within the next year or so, and immediately again began the struggle for independence.

The casualties of the rebellion have officially been listed as the following:

British forces	-	132 killed	397 wounded
Irish Rebels and Civilians	-	318 killed	2197 wounded

Towards Independence

As previously mentioned, Sinn Fein had pretty much given way during the Easter Rising to the more aggressive elements of the Physical Force Party, and as an organization Sinn Fein had not been officially involved. It now however seized upon the political opportunities and won a number of important elections in 1917. One of those winning a seat in parliament from the region of east Clare was Eamon de Valera, the only surviving commandant of the Easter Rising. His platform was that of the proclamation of 1916, and he won by a substantial margin. By the end of 1917, he had replaced Arthur Griffith as the leader of the reorganized Sinn Fein party (remember it was originally Arthur Griffith's party and he envisioned something of a dual monarchy similar to that of Austria-Hungary—it was now the party of the republican revolutionaries); and, in the general elections of 1918, Sinn Fein won seventy-three of the Irish seats in parliament and the Unionists won twenty-six.

The British government most likely underestimated the popular support behind the Sinn Fein party, and the party's potential growth and strength. This, combined with the fact that world opinion, and especially that of the United States, had taken a hard line in condemning the British executions of 1916, led Britain to adopt a policy of leniency towards the Irish. Most of the rebels that had been interned and imprisoned following the Easter Rising, and expected to receive life sentences, were released by Christmas of 1916.

In 1918, the members of the Sinn Fein party refused to take their Parliamentary seats in Westminster, instead calling for an all-Irish parliament to meet in Dublin during January of 1919. They in fact did meet in Dublin on the twenty-first of January and formed the Dail Eireann (Assembly of Ireland), without thirty-six elected Sinn Fein delegates who were in jail. The structure and particulars of the Dail Eireann had been finalized by late 1918 in preparation, initiated immediately after 9 April 1918, when the British Prime Minister Lloyd George announced a plan for military conscription of Irish citizens. (Conscription was never imposed but was often mentioned until the end of the war.) In early 1918

Eamon de Valera had been arrested and jailed as Sinn Fein, the Physical Force Party, the Irish Republican Brotherhood, and the Irish Volunteers (who had now become the military wing of the Sinn Fein party), had all been declared illegal, but within a year he escaped from Lincoln Jail in England (with the help of Michael Collins and Harry Boland) and was elected president of the Dail Eireann in April of 1919. Shortly thereafter, he left for America to both raise funds and seek American support for "The Republic". He then also went to the Peace Conference at Versailles seeking support and recognition for The Irish Republic.

The Dail Eireann declared Ireland a Republic as defined by the proclamation of 1916, professed their sole authority to pass legislation binding Irish citizens, and demanded the immediate evacuation of Ireland by the English garrison. This of course meant the entire island, but the British government had now been committed to partition as proposed before the war. The "Northern Ireland" territory would consist of six counties, originally defined by Edward Carson and the Unionists, after their executive officers determined this was the maximum territory they could possibly hold. The British government also refused to grant any additional powers to the twenty-six "Southern Ireland" counties, other than those granted by the Home Rule Bill of 1912.

It was becoming evident that Ireland and England were again heading towards war. The Irish Republican Army (the reorganized Volunteers) was now carrying out successful attacks against British troops and police. The I.R.A. probably never numbered more than fifteen thousand individuals at that time, armed with pistols, rifles, and shotguns. They faced great odds as the British military forces under General Macready numbered over forty-five thousand men armed with the latest military equipment. The leader of this Irish activity was for the most part Michael Collins, who had fought in the General Post Office during 1916, and was a master of intelligence, tactics and organization. British paid informants had hurt the Irish cause for independence in the past and Michael Collins was masterful at not only clearing these from the Irish ranks, but also placing Irish informants among the British administration at Dublin Castle. Over two and a half years of guerrilla warfare ensued.

In March of 1920, the British reinforced their police, The Royal Irish Constabulary, with a force comprised of ex-soldiers and prisoners who carried the nickname of "Black and Tans", because they wore a uniform that was a combination of both the police and army uniforms. The Black and Tans were joined in

Ireland, in August 1920 by the Auxiliaries, a group of ex-British army officers. Both of these groups engaged in hundreds of atrocities perpetrated against the Irish including torture, murder, dismemberment, burning, and rape. They were extremely undisciplined, brutal, and violent. The British once again instituted a program of mass internment in August of 1920 after parliament passed the "Restotation of Order to Ireland Act". In response to these actions, the Irish Republican Army was forced to ban together for the protection of the people, and remain as anonymous as possible. The Irish Republican Army's "Flying Columns" were formed during this period and carried out a quite successful campaign of counterattacks and ambushes against the Black and Tan, Auxiliary, and R.I.C. forces, especially between September 1920 and April 1921.

Through Michael Collins' intricate network of informers he was able to mysteriously mastermind the jailbreaks of numerous Irish political prisoners, while at the same time also miraculously evading arrest when the British were certain they had him. He was so elusive the British weren't even certain of exactly what he looked like. He was Director of Intelligence for the I.R.A. and was extremely proficient at identifying and assassinating key figures of the Detective Division of both the Royal Irish Constabulary and the Dublin Metropolitan Police (there known as the "G Division"), as well as many of the leaders and more violent members of the Auxiliaries and the Black and Tans. Four main recruits within the G Division of the Dublin Metropolitan Police kept Collins informed of all police and government activities—Kavanagh, MacNamara, Neligan, and Broy. Broy was appointed the Commissioner of the Garda Siochana in 1933. By the end of 1920 his "Murder Squad" (known irreverently within the I.R.A. as the "Twelve Apostles") had rendered British Intelligence impotent, and Michael Collins was the most wanted man in Ireland with a bounty on his head of 10,000 pounds. For the first time in the seven hundred year history of Irish repression, Irish Intelligence was superior to the long-established and arrogant British Intelligence Service.

The "Irish War of Independence" (contrary to many popular accounts, there was never a declaration of war in January 1919 following the killing of two constables down in County Tipperary) resulted in less than twenty deaths in 1919, less than three hundred deaths in 1920 (with another 100 killed in Ulster sectarian violence), but nearly 1100 were killed in 1921 before the truce was signed. Approximately half of all killed were soldiers and/or policemen. Many of the Large Houses of the more oppressive English landlords were burned down as well. The Irish Republican Army possessed the overwhelming popular support of the Irish people (with many popular citizen heroes such as Dan Breen, Tom Barry and Liam Lynch), and could easily disappear into the population before and after operations. In response, the British initiated an even more violent policy of counter-terrorism that again horrified those around the world, including many in Britain.

One particular day that raised the anger on both sides to a fevered pitch was 21 November 1920, known as "Bloody Sunday". The British had brought their own assassination squad (known as the "Cairo Gang") into Dublin to assassinate Michael Collins and other leading members of the I.R.A. They attempted to live among the ordinary citizens but were quickly identified by Collins' network. That Sunday morning, Collins' Murder Squad assassinated eleven members of the Cairo Gang. In the afternoon squads of Black and Tans burst into Croke Park during a hurling match between Dublin and Tipperary, and fired into the crowd. Twelve people were killed, including one player, and over sixty people were wounded.

One week later, the flying column of Commandant Tom Barry's No. 3 Cork Brigade ambushed a large convoy of Auxiliaries near Kilmichael in County Cork, killing all but one man. On 11 December 1920, County Cork was placed under Martial Law. That night a large portion of Cork City was burnt to the ground by the Auxiliaries and the Black and Tans, who then wore burnt corks in their caps to commemorate their achievement.

The I.R.A. and the Irish people held out long enough under these extremely adverse conditions to make the British program of repression a political burden for the English government. The Lord Mayor of Cork, Terence MacSwiney, died in October of 1920 following a seventy-five day hunger strike, and this became one of many profound symbols indicating Irish resistance. Irish resolve was also reinforced by the great quantities of funds and support coming in from America.

David Lloyd George, the British Prime Minister, then drafted the "Government of Ireland Act" which became law before the end of 1920. It provided for Parliaments to be established in both Dublin and Ulster. "Northern Ireland" would consist of the six counties of Antrim, Armagh, Derry, Down, Fermanagh, and Tyrone. "Southern Ireland" would include the remaining twenty-six counties of Carlow, Cavan, Clare, Cork, Donegal, Dublin, Galway, Kerry, Kildare, Kilkenny, Laois, Leitrim, Limerick, Longford, Louth, Mayo, Meath, Monaghan, Offaly, Roscommon, Sligo, Tipperary, Waterford, Westmeath, Wexford, and Wicklow. In the "North" Unionists won forty of the fifty-two seats contested in the May 1921 elections. In the "South", Sinn Fein ran unopposed in 124 of the 128 seats. The remaining four seats were allocated to Unionists representing the University of Dublin (including Trinity College). These two governments were formed and the Irish War for Independence officially ended on 11 July 1921, one day before Britain, according to the Government of Ireland Act, was to impose martial law in Ireland and force Ireland to become a colony of the British Crown.

The treaty negotiations now began in London and lasted almost five months. The British delegation's leader was Prime Minister David Lloyd George and the Irish delegation's leaders were Arthur Griffith and Michael Collins. Eamon de Valera had remained in Dublin, professing that this was his proper place, establishing the new Irish government, when in fact he knew the Irish delegates position was tenuous and they would be most likely unable to secure the concessions desired by the majority of the Irish people. After much argument, and quite proficient and astute bargaining by the Irish delegation, the "Articles of Agreement for a Treaty between Great Britain and Ireland" was drawn up on 6 December 1921, and signed by the Irish delegation under the threat of the immediate resumption of war by a frustrated Lloyd George. Griffith and Collins had in fact secured substantial concessions in very important areas, such as defense, tariffs, taxation, commerce, policing, and nomenclature. Many of these they would not have predicted achieving originally. They thought they had done well, providing a giant stepping-stone from which further unity, independence, and self-government could be attained.

A personal meeting between Michael Collins and Prime Minister Lloyd George on the morning of 5 December determined much of the form and content of the Treaty's Articles. The Anglo-Irish Treaty provided that the new "Irish Free State" would govern itself, have dominion status (similar to that of Canada and Australia), that its members of the Irish Parliament must swear an oath of allegiance to the British crown (Collins won a big concession here regarding the wording of the oath. The Irish MP's were to swear a primary oath to the Constitution of the Irish Free State first, and thereafter faithfulness to the British monarchy). Collins also achieved his major concession, total independence for the Irish Army. Britain however would be allowed to maintain certain defensive naval bases in the port cities of Cobh, Berehaven, and Lough Swilley. Northern Ireland was given the opportunity to "opt out" of this new Irish Free State if it so desired. The Parliament in Belfast immediately took advantage of this clause. There was also a Boundary Commission established to "adjust the existing border in accordance to the wishes of the inhabitants, so far as may be compatible with economic and geographic conditions".

The Irish treaty delegates returned to Dublin, and the Dail Eireann became at once divided as to whether or not they should accept the terms of the treaty. Eamon de Valera was adamant about not swearing an oath of allegiance. Collins and Griffith believed they had secured the very best terms possible under the circumstances, and Michael Collins told the Dail that their delegation, "had not received the ultimate freedom that all nations aspire and develop to, but had received the freedom to achieve it". Most of the Irish people greeted the news of this treaty with great joy and immense relief, as the British army and the hated Black and Tans would finally leave and go home. Interestingly enough, partition of the island did not receive a great deal of attention in these early debates. Most people seemed to believe this was a most temporary phenomenon as the Boundary Commission would surely take note of the wishes of the Catholic majorities in counties Tyrone and Fermanagh. This would only leave four counties in Northern Ireland, and these could certainly never survive long as an independent political nor economic unit. The Dail Eireann voted by a count of sixty-four votes to fifty-seven votes on 7 January 1922, to accept the treaty.

Eamon de Valera immediately resigned as President and was replaced by Arthur Griffith. On the sixteenth of January, a provisional government under the leadership of Michael Collins took possession of Dublin Castle, and the withdrawal of British troops and administrators was begun. De Valera sought a revision of the treaty but when the Dail Eireann voted against him in late January, the Irish Republican Army split nearly in half, some seeing the treaty as the stepping-stone to achieve the Republic, and the other half viewing it as nothing but treason to the ideals of the Republic and they vowed to fight onward. The two groups each took control of various buildings within Dublin and elsewhere.

The two Irish factions, the pro-treaty "Free Staters" and the anti-treaty "Republicans", were widely divided and adamantly opposed to each other's position. The strongest opposition to the treaty came from the south and west, from such counties as Cork, Tipperary, Kilkenny, and Wexford. In March and April of 1922, a group of anti-treaty dissidents calling themselves the "Irregulars" pledged allegiance to the Republic of 1916, and occupied the Four Courts, the Dublin Judicial Building, and a few other minor buildings, turning them into fortified positions. General elections were to be held on the sixteenth of June, so no immediate action was taken hoping the elections would provide a solution that would be honored by all. In the elections, only thirty-six seats out of one hundred and twenty-eight went to anti-treaty republicans.

Approximately a week later the Irregulars occupying the Four Courts abducted a pro-treaty general, and Michael Collins ordered an attack on the building. On 26 June 1922, Free State troops opened fire on the Four Courts with big guns they had borrowed from the British and the Irish Civil War had begun. Two days later, over one hundred Irregulars in the Four Courts surrendered.

On 12 August of that year, an extremely dismayed and exhausted Arthur Griffith died unexpectedly. Ten days later Michael Collins was killed in an ambush down in Beal na mBlath, County Cork, and this action deeply embittered both sides, as all had deep respect for Michael Collins. During the next couple of months seventy-seven Republican prisoners were executed. By October of 1922, the pro-treaty Free Staters had secured control of all the major cities and most of the countryside.

In September 1922, the new Dail Eireann met under heavy guard and began the process of writing a "Free State Constitution". William Cosgrave became president of the Dail, and Kevin O'Higgins became vice-president and Minister of Justice. From 1923 until 1927, the Republicans, and their party Fianna Fail, organized in 1926, did not acknowledge this Dail Eireann, would not take the oath of allegiance, and would not take their seats in this Dail. During this period, with virtually no opposition party, the Dail Eireann established a new police force, a permanent army, put through several measures to aid Irish agriculture and industry, and implemented a plan to harness the River Shannon as a source of power. The huge success of the Shannon River Project demonstrated to people the benefits of peaceful pursuit of progress. Fianna Fail was often portrayed as simply a front for violent revolutionaries whose object it was to overthrow the state, but de Valera disassociated the party from all violence and began working through political and constitutional means to build a strong political base.

In 1924, the Boundary Commission was organized as provided for by the treaty. Northern Ireland refused to appoint a delegate (just as they have done with the Good Friday Agreement) and swore not to yield one inch of ground. Eoin MacNeill, a Professor of Irish History, was the delegate appointed by the Free State and after attending several worthless meetings, resigned in disgust. No changes were ever made in the boundary. Eamon de Valera always criticized this partition, as did so many others, as a direct result of the 1921 treaty, and he began a political campaign to reverse this under the auspices of the political party Fianna Fail (Warriors, or Soldiers, of Destiny), founded in 1926. Cosgrave's party was known as the Cumann na nGaedheal, later becoming simply the Fine Gael (Tribe of Gaels). There was always the question among the people as to exactly how sovereign Ireland was in reality, especially with the British ports on Irish soil. What if Britain became involved in another great war—would Ireland be safe? The stability was further questioned following the assassination of Kevin O'Higgins, the Minister of Justice who had served in the original Dail Eireann and founded the unarmed Irish National Police Force, the Garda Siochana.

Over fierce opposition from the British, the Irish Free State succeeded in gaining a seat in the League of Nations, and established diplomatic relations with a number of other nations. Great progress was made during the Cosgrave administration, including the 1931 fight for the "Statute of Westminster", which recognized the unquestionable authority of each of Britain's several dominions to legislate for themselves in all sovereign matters.

In the general election of 1932, Fianna Fail won seventy-two out of one hundred and fifty-three seats, making it the majority party; and, with the support of the Labour Party, Eamon de Valera organized a new government. Over the next forty years, Fianna Fail would only be out of office for six short years (1948-1951 and 1954-1957). Eamon de Valera immediately abolished the oath of allegiance, and attempted to sever all other ties possible with Great Britain. De Valera always hesitated to declare, or even term, Ireland a "Republic", because he believed she could never be so without her "Fourth Green Field" (Ulster, or the six counties of the North). Instead, in 1937, he devised and had enacted a new "Consitution of Ireland", which in fact laid claim to all the island's national territory, but limited its jurisdiction to the twenty-six counties "pending the re-integration of the national territory". This provoked great anger and fury from both Britain and the Ulster Unionists, whose Parliament even then considered changing the name of Northern Ireland to the State, or Country, of Ulster.

Great Britain had initiated a number of severe economic reprisals following the beginning of de Valera's constitutional efforts and the dropping of the oath of fidelity. Fianna Fail then also employed protectionist economic policies eventually leading to a six-year economic war with Great Britain, ending in 1938. Trade was resumed slowly between the two after April 1938, when Prime Minister Chamberlain appeased the Irish by settling disputes regarding annuities and punitive debt; and, by surrendering the naval bases in Irish ports that had been allowed by the Anglo-Irish Treaty. The Free State had won concessions, but all the while Northern Ireland was far more rapidly developing in economic terms, primarily due to British government agricultural subsidies and the favored British trade status given the North during the economic war.

Fianna Fail had from the start ignored Britain's Governor General for Ireland, and after several unsuccessful rebuffs and protests, he resigned the position. A member of Fianna Fail assumed the post for a few years until the position was abolished in 1938.

Fianna Fail made passionate efforts to restore the Irish culture, history and pride. Irish was declared the "first official language" in the 1937 constitution, subsidies were given to major "Gaelteacht" regions and, in opposition to British censorship, promoted an Irish-language counter-culture that produced some of the finest Irish writings of all time. (The English language would always have its place in Ireland, as many young Irish still looked to the glamour and possibilities of study and work abroad.)

The Irish Constitution, which took effect on 29 December 1937, called the "Bunreacht na hEireann", is rather unique in many principles. It declared Ireland to be a free, independent, sovereign and democratic state with the people supplying all power and being the final arbiters on all matters. It recognized the family as the natural unit of society, and forbade divorce. It guaranteed all freedoms of conscience and religion. The community-held resources were to be distributed equally throughout society. And it acknowledged God as the ultimate source of all authority.

The constitution provides for a two-chamber Irish Parliament (Oireachtas), the Dail Eireann (members are called T.D.'s—Teachta Dalas, or Deputies) and the Seanad Eireann (members are called Senators) with a President of Ireland

(Uachtaran na hEireann), elected by a direct vote of the people. The Taoiseach is elected by the Parliament. I believe it was previously mentioned that the national territory was defined to include the thirty-two counties of Ireland, but until "re-integration", the jurisdiction of the Irish Parliament was limited to the twenty-six counties. The Republic was officially named "Eire" (the Irish word for the island), and in English it was to be called Ireland.

Tony Finnegan gives a lesson in Irish.

Ireland remained neutral throughout World War II, although several of the combatants, including the United States, thought about invading the island. The United States had actually devised a plan to do so and came within a couple of weeks of implementing it, but I suppose this just never became necessary from a standpoint of strategic importance. Britain had a rather large naval base at Derry (now called Londonderry) in Northern Ireland, and from there protected her western coast without infringing upon the Free State. Reclaiming the old British naval bases had also been rather strongly considered by both the United States and Britain but was never acted upon. There is some evidence that Winston Churchill, the British Prime Minister, promised that if Ireland fought for the Allies, he would introduce legislation to unify Ireland. There is no indication that Eamon de Valera ever acted upon this information, probably for a variety of reasons.

Through this period, Fianna Fail, remained easily the largest political party, but several smaller political parties were organizing, such as the "Clann na Poblachta", or Republican Family. This party was founded and led by Sean MacBride, a handsome dashing soldier and the son of Robert MacBride, who was executed in 1916, and the beautiful actress Maud Gonne. He had also been a former Chief of Staff of the I.R.A. In 1948, many of these minor parties formed a coalition with the Fine Gael party and the Labour party; and, Fine Gael's John A. Costello became Taoiseach. Before the end of the year they had passed the "Republic of Ireland Act", which severed the last constitutional links with Britain, and the Republic of Ireland was officially inaugurated on Easter Monday, 1949. Eamon de Valera pointed out that in 1916, they had been fighting for an all-Ireland Republic, and he would take no part in the inaugural ceremonies whatsoever. Shortly thereafter, the English parliament passed the "Ireland Act", which stated that no part of Northern Ireland would ever leave His Majesty's dominion without the approval of the Parliament of Northern Ireland (a major reason the Unionists of Northern Ireland will seat no delegates currently in the power sharing Northern Ireland Assembly provided for in the Good Friday Agreement of 1998).

The Irish inter-party government of Labour, Fine Gael, and Clann na Poblachta broke up in 1951, following a controversy over a scheme providing free health care for expectant mothers and children, proposed by Dr. Noel Browne, as well as other social issues, many centered around involvement between church and state as John Costello had conferred with the Catholic Archbishop of Dublin regarding a couple of matters. The inter-party government's greatest achievements domestically came in the areas of public health and health care, although Ireland still lagged behind most of Europe in these areas. There was also another inter-party government from 1954 to 1957. It broke up when Clann na Poblachta withdrew because the government had no clear plan for the re-unification of Ireland, nor effective economic policies. (See Appendix F—Political Makeup of the 29th Dail)

Fianna Fail again took control in 1957, and in 1959, Eamon de Valera was elected to the above-politics symbolic office of President of Ireland. He represented a great living link to the heroic politics of 1916. Sean Lemass, who had fought in the G.P.O. in 1916, became the Taoiseach and under his direction Ireland began a period of rapid economic expansion.

Sean Lemass mostly set aside the issue of re-unification and began a good neighbor policy with the North. In 1965, he traveled to Belfast to meet with the Northern Ireland Prime Minister, Captain Terence O'Neill. This was the first time the two Irish factions had met in negotiations since the early 1920's, and it looked as if the relationship might progress; however, as we all know there was still an extremely rocky road ahead. Both Sean Lemass and Terence O'Neill were heavily criticized at home for this meeting. It in effect cost O'Neill his political career. (Several successive Irish governments, even to this very day, have sought to develop a solution to the problems and provide lasting peace and stability, but sentiments continue to run deep on both sides—perhaps soon.)

Ireland at that time also began to look outward and develop relationships within the world community. In 1955, Ireland was admitted to the United Nations and from 1958 onward Irish troops have served in several United Nations' peacekeeping missions. In 1965, Irish soldiers fought for the first time with the United Nations forces. From 1957 to 1961 the Minister for Foreign Affairs, Mr. Frank Aiken, was known within the United Nations as a strong independent attempting to reduce cold-war tensions. From 1951 to 1969 Irish politics were rather uneventful as domestic and economic concerns were addressed, and Ireland often looked westward strengthening ties with America. In 1973, Ireland officially became a member of the European Economic Community.

In Northern Ireland both the government and society seemed to evolve quite differently than it had in The Irish Free State, later to become The Republic of Ireland. The Protestant/Unionist minority in The Republic only numbered about five percent and readily accepted the ways and institutions of The Republic. In the North however, the Catholic/Nationalist minority numbered more than a third of the population in 1921 (today it represents approximately half), and possessed vast majorities of the population in some areas—particularly in cities like Derry, and along the border with The Republic, with whom they were known to share common sympathies. I.R.A. ploughboys could expect assistance on both sides of the border and the North knew this and always viewed the Catholic population with contempt and suspicion. Many of these Catholic/Nationalist people were neither yet ready to accept partition nor the one-sided oppressive institutions of Northern Ireland. Protestant/Unionist fear of a Catholic/Nationalist revolution and backlash has basically provided the platform for the Unionist parties' politics in Northern Ireland ever since (The primary example being Ian Paisley's Ulster Democratic Unionist Party, which evolved from his Protestant

Unionist Party), and has gained the Unionists huge support amongst the Protestant community, and has in reality perpetuated a division that has caused pain and suffering to millions.

In nearly all religions, there is a minority of those misrepresenting the religion and using it for personal gain or power, be it political, economic, military, or to simply win an argument, whatever. All religions appear to promote love, compassion, understanding, forgiveness, patience, and peaceful coexistence. It is amazing the numbers of people that have followed those perpetuating anger, hatred, violence, abuse—all in the name of the Lord or the One True God. Throughout history there are numerous examples. Oliver Cromwell comes to mind immediately in Ireland.

Ian Paisley was mentioned earlier along with the fact he has perpetuated an extremely angry, violent, and hateful atmosphere while preaching on Sundays about peace and love. His fiery rhetoric has encouraged a dangerous situation in which many have suffered, on both sides, and it has been a continuous obstacle to peace and a source of sad concern for all in Ireland, Britain, and America—all with a holier-than-thou arrogance assuring the maintenance of the anger he promotes. He was born on 6 April 1926, the son of a Baptist minister who had served in Carson's Ulster Volunteers in 1912. He attended a technical secondary school, with his only other formal education being at the Reformed Presbyterian Theological Hall in Belfast. In 1966 he was given, quite interestingly, an honorary doctorate degree from Bob Jones University in America. In 1946 he was ordained a minister in the Free Presbyterian Church and erected a church called the Martyrs Memorial Free Presbyterian Church, at Ravenhill in Belfast. He has been there ever since.

In the mid-fifties he founded the reactionary group called the Ulster Protestant Volunteers, in name reverting back to pre World War I days. He was arrested twice for his street speeches and politics promoting hatred and instilling great fear in a helpless Northern Ireland Catholic minority. The Provisional IRA was organized as the initial response in an effort to protect the Catholic people. Paisley was elected to the UK Parliament in 1970 from North Antrim, a rural agricultural very conservative region, and in 1971 along with several others, founded the Ulster Democratic Unionist Party which he stills leads today.

He made a dramatic resignation from his North Antrim seat in 1985 following the signing of the Anglo-Irish agreement, the only positive political progress at that point yet made in Ulster. He has lobbied against any dialogue or cooperation between the two communities, and to this day is utilizing every political tool possible to prevent implementation of the 1998 Belfast Agreement and the power sharing Northern Ireland Assembly, which over 90% of the people have favored in referendum. Ian Paisley preaches, and firmly believes, all Catholics are doomed and the Pope in Rome is the anti-Christ spoken about by St. John the Divine. Despite his perpetuation of anger and hatred he has been the highest polling politician in Northern Ireland, yet he still represents an increasingly shrinking minority view. Too many seem to preach hatred and division in the name of the Lord Jesus Christ, who himself only spoke of love and the need for all inclusive unity among men!

Modern Ireland

The Euro and the Republic of Ireland's inclusion in the European Union has dramatically changed the country and built it up in a way that could have never been imagined only a few years ago. When Ireland first entered the European Union it was among the poorest countries, and now thanks to the Celtic Tiger and the influx of companies dealing in information technologies, Ireland is among the wealthiest countries in the European Union. The progress and future potential are staggering.

This however has also led to some dramatic changes in the landscape and population. The building of large homes and factories has changed the look of peaceful tranquil rural Ireland nearly everywhere. In Dublin massive cranes dot the skyline and construction activity is highly visible in all sectors. Immigrants from many of the poorer countries of the European Union have flocked to Ireland for increased opportunities and a better lifestyle, hence the makeup of the once rather homogenous Irish population is rapidly changing. Many native sons are returning home as well, and the migratory and economic movement across the border with Northern Ireland has also changed dramatically. The armed border crossings of only a few years ago are all gone now.

World War II had somewhat alienated the Republic of Ireland from Northern Ireland. The Republic had remained neutral during the conflict while Northern Ireland had been extensively bombed, as it was considered a member of the Allied Forces. On one day alone, the fourth of May 1941, 204 German planes dropped over 95,000 bombs on the harbor and shipyards of Belfast, virtually destroying both and rendering them totally unusable. England was then forced to utilize the ports and naval yards of Derry (now called by the British, Londonderry). Britain had helped build up Northern Ireland's industry to support the war effort; and, following the war helped rebuild where needed. Britain also helped establish and maintain governmental institutions in Northern Ireland.

The mysterious barman of Inishmurray Island.

At the time the Republic of Ireland was founded in 1949, the main goals there seemed to be focused on the formation of the new government and the establishment of associated services, along with the settling of political differences among the various factions. It would be approximately ten years before the first serious economic and industrialization programs could be addressed. Hence, at that time the economic conditions (i.e. Per capita income, Gross National Product, Balance of Trade, etc.) were developing more rapidly in the North. However, their lack of addressing the basic political problems and differences would dramatically devastate their economy on down the road.

Let's discuss briefly some of the major events and factors influencing the evolution of Northern Ireland since its inception in 1921. When King George V of England opened the new Northern Ireland Parliament in June of 1921 he pleaded with all Irishmen to, "pause, to stretch out the hand of forbearance and conciliation, to forgive and forget, and to join in making for the land they love a new era of peace, contentment and conciliation". Well, apparently not many were listening, as the years of Northern Ireland "home rule" (1921-1972) were marked by incredible violence and tension, as both the majority Unionists and the minority Nationalists resented each other's role in society.

The mostly Catholic Nationalists had virtually no role in government and suffered great systematic discrimination in many areas, including voting rights, housing and employment. There were generations of poorer Irish being born, living their entire lives, and dying without ever holding a proper job, and people not only need jobs to support their families, they need jobs to promote hope and dignity. They came to deeply resent what they saw as an unnatural and obtrusive partition of the island; and, the mostly Protestant Unionists took an extremely defensive position swearing to never surrender an inch. The Catholics/Nationalists were also reluctant to support or become a part of the institutions they hoped would not survive.

The initial sectarian violence lasted through 1922, leading to the "Special Powers Acts of 1922—1933. The virtually all-protestant Northern Ireland Police Force, the Royal Ulster Constabulary, was reinforced with the virtually all-protestant Auxiliaries and the Ulster Special Constabulary. These organizations were violently oppressive to Catholics, leading to deep-rooted hatreds and of course dividing the two factions even further.

Also in 1922, the Unionists abolished proportional representation and redrew several boundaries to insure their continued control of most all the local and statewide political councils. (This is when the Unionists gained control of Derry, as up until this time, Derry had always been controlled by Nationalists.) From then on, the Unionists had no problem maintaining a sizeable majority in the Parliament of Northern Ireland at Stormont.

Rioting and sectarian violence heightened again in 1935, when the Northern Ireland government banned all parades and marches (in a supposed effort to quell violence), and then lifted the ban in July, allowing the Orange Order to conduct their marches and celebrations.

British financial support of the institutions of Northern Ireland also led to further divisions, with the Protestant/Unionist majority enjoying a substantially higher standard of living as the result of basically the establishment of a British welfare state. The Unionists then became even more defensive, and often oppressive, in an effort to maintain this "favored" status. These actions directly led to a heightened anti-partition campaign by the Irish Republican Army, especially after the establishment of The Republic in 1949. These efforts increased dramatically between the years of 1955 and 1962.

In 1963, Captain Terence O'Neill succeeded Sir Basil Brooke as Prime Minister of Northern Ireland. He was the first Prime Minister having not been directly influenced by the events and circumstances of the early 1920's, and he tried honestly to draw the Catholics into the mainstream of Ulster social and political life. These efforts drew great anger and criticism from the Unionists who feared the rising Catholic population would soon vote Northern Ireland into the Republic of Ireland. His most outspoken opponent was of course the Reverend Ian Paisley of the rather small "Free Presbyterian Church". Opposition to O'Neill's policies was building even within his own party, and increased dramatically after his 1965 meeting with Sean Lemass, the Taoiseach of the Irish Republic. Catholic Civil Rights movements had been increasing steadily in the 1960's, surely following the patterns set in America, and when a Civil Rights March was banned in Derry in October 1968, leading to violence throughout the city, O'Neill was heavily criticized and forced to resign early in 1969.

His successor, Major James Chichester-Clark, was no more successful in stopping the violence. In August 1969, a parade organized by the Orange Order and commemorating the defense of Derry against James II in the year 1690, was attacked by Irish Nationalists. This was followed by virtual all-out warfare in the area of the Catholic Bogside. This led to violence elsewhere in Northern Ireland and eventually the British Army was brought in to restore calm. Following the British government's advisement, the government of Northern Ireland began instituting minor reforms.

The Irish Republican Army saw this as the ideal time to bring down the Stormont government. The I.R.A.'s power and influence had increased substantially as they had acted as the defenders of the Nationalist neighborhoods, especially in Belfast and Derry. The I.R.A. had become ever more hostile towards the British occupying military forces, and had established "no go" areas in Belfast and Derry, areas in which the police and British forces were not permitted to enter.

Just as their power and ideals were being recognized, philosophical differences led to a division within the I.R.A. The "Official I.R.A.", which was based on the Marxist ideologies of socialized control, broke away from the "Provisional I.R.A." which was more traditional and based on the Revolution of 1916. Both factions continued the fight against partition and British military occupation, and Chichester-Clark resigned in 1971, when the British government refused to step up their attacks on the I.R.A. (Note: Today there are several splinter factions calling themselves I.R.A., many are basically self-proclaiming groups attempting to perpetuate their particular views and/or ideologies.)

The rioting and violence continued to escalate, and the Dail Eireann debated day and night what had happened and exactly which policies it should pursue, in an effort to reverse these extremely bitter feelings that had not been seen since the 1920's. The I.R.A.'s campaign to basically bring down the government of Northern Ireland reached such an intensity in 1971, that this government, with the reluctant support of Britain, initiated internment without trial. Over three hundred persons were arrested and interned. The rioting that followed internment was among the worst ever and forced thousands living in "mixed" neighborhoods to flee their homes creating the drastically misnamed "Peace Lines", many of which in Belfast and Derry remain to this day.

An event that radicalized the Nationalist community more than any other was the second "Bloody Sunday" killings of thirteen Nationalist demonstrators by the British Army in January 1972 during a Civil Rights March. The Nationalist community's feelings were best represented at that time through the uncharacteristic words of John Hume, leader of the Socialist and Democratic Labor Party, "Many people feel now that is a united Ireland or nothing". The hopeful beliefs of the Civil Rights Era had in a good part faded and the British Army, once welcomed as protection for the Nationalist community from the violence of the Loyalists, was now viewed as the enemy. Black flags of mourning and anger were flown everywhere, and many previously uninvolved people were now drawn through bitter emotionalism towards the I.R.A. and the Republican movement.

In March 1972, the British government did in fact suspend the Stormont Parliament and government, basically in direct response to Bloody Sunday. This was originally to be for one year and the hopes were that, with the Unionists out of power, the battle-weary Nationalists would turn to measures of conciliation and turn away from the I.R.A. However, the backlash from angry Protestants, who now distrusted the British government and became even more militant and violent, only strengthened the position of the I.R.A.

In 1973, the British government published a White Paper in which they proposed a new "Northern Ireland Assembly", in which Catholics and Protestants would share governmental powers that were somewhat more limited than the powers enjoyed by the Stormont government.

Brian Faulkner and the Unionist Party very reluctantly agreed to the new government, reckoning some control over local affairs would be better than none at all. They further expected that I.R.A. suspects held in the Republic of Ireland would be extradited to Northern Ireland for trial; and, Articles 2 and 3 of the 1937 Constitution of Ireland, claiming sovereignty over the counties of Northern Ireland would be changed. Northern Ireland Nationalists and the Republic of Ireland government, on the other hand, wanted a strong All-Ireland institution, that would grow dramatically in power and scope leading eventually to a United Ireland. They also sought reform at that time of the Royal Ulster Constabulary (R.U.C.), the Unionist controlled police force of Northern Ireland.

Elections were held on 28 June 1973, based on proportional representation, and a coalition government was organized at Sunningdale, England, in December of 1973, and was to be called the "Council of Ireland". It took office on 1 January 1974, and from the beginning was undermined by the Unionists who saw it as an attempt to unify Northern Ireland with the Republic. The British General Elections held in early 1973 saw the Pro-Sunningdale Unionists soundly defeated (achieving only 13% of the vote), and the coalition government then collapsed in the face of a Protestant workers' strike, organized by the Ulster Workers' Council, in May of that year. In 1976, the Unionists proposed a "Constitutional Convention", basically an effort to assure their continued privileged status, but it found rejection from both the British and the Irish governments immediately.

Levels of violence and conflict fluctuated over the next several years. The Northern Ireland police force (the Royal Ulster Constabulary) was strengthened and every time they would attempt to exert an increased authority, it would bring reprisals from the Irish Republican Army. Since the late 1970's, the British have attempted to steadily diminish the roles of both their military and their political influence. Internment, the holding of suspected members of the I.R.A. without trial and/or the trial without jury for suspected terrorist offenses, which was introduced in 1971, ended in 1975.

Irish Republican prisoners began calling world attention to the situation beginning in the late seventies, by demanding status as "political prisoners". They employed many tactics, but gained world recognition through their "hunger strikes". In 1981, ten prisoners died during a hunger strike, including Bobby Sands, who, while imprisoned and dying, was elected to the British Parliament at Westminster, as a representative from the Counties of Fermanagh and South Tyrone.

The Hunger Strike is an ancient Irish Celtic method of fighting injustices. It was codified in the early Celtic Brehon Laws and could be employed as a solution for solving both personal and social wrongdoings. The law provided that if someone was intentionally done wrong by another, he would publicly state the fact and then present himself on the perpetrator's doorstep and begin the fasting. This would hopefully shame, or scare, the perpetrator into righting the wrong. If the plaintiff starved to death, the one responsible had to pay great indemnities to the dead man's family and support them for the remainder of their lives. It was also believed the perpetrator would be subjected to horrific supernatural penalties. This process in Irish is known as "Toscad".

Twenty-two Irish Martyrs have died since 1917, as a result of "Toscad Poblachta" (Political or Republican Hunger Strikes), initiated to call attention to British oppression. These are (from earliest to most recent) Thomas Ashe, Michael Fitzgerald, Joseph Murphy, Terrence MacSwiney (who was the Lord Mayor of Cork), Joseph Whitty, Denis Barry, Andy Sullivan, Tony D'Arcy, Sean McNeela, Sean McCaughey, Michael Gaughan, Frank Stagg, Bobby Sands, Francis Hughes, Ray McCreesh, Patsy O'Hara, Joe McDonnell, Martin Hurson, Kevin Lynch, Kieran Doherty, Tom McElwee, and Michael Devine. (Metress, 1983)

In 1985, the Anglo-Irish Agreement was another effort to provide Northern Ireland with a National Constitution. The Republic of Ireland agreed to be available for consultation, triggering a violent and angry reaction from the Unionist Party and Ian Paisley's Ulster Democratic Unionist Party, claiming this was just another attempt at re-unification of Northern Ireland and the Republic of Ireland. In response to the violent backlash from the Unionists, the I.R.A. brought in their largest cache of weapons in history, securing many from Libya and Colonel Moamar Qadaffi. These included AK 47's, Russian made machine guns, SAM 7 Rocket Launchers, and large quantities of semtex explosives manufactured in Czechoslovakia (an odorless and nearly undetectable explosive used in virtually every I.R.A. mission since 1986). These materials have been the focus of the decommissioning talks associated with the Belfast Agreement. If there was one major positive outcome of the 1985 Anglo-Irish Agreement, it was an apparent increase in communication and trust between the governments of Britain and the Republic of Ireland.

In 1998, on Good Friday, the Belfast Agreement was devised to eventually lead again to Northern Ireland "Home Rule". In May 1999, the Agreement received the approval of the Irish people in simultaneous referendums held in both the Republic and Northern Ireland. Powers were to be devolved by Britain and shared by a cabinet comprised of members from the four largest political parties (two Nationalist, the Social Democratic and Labour Party and the Sinn Fein Party; and, two Unionist, the Ulster Unionist Party and the Ulster Democratic Unionist Party), but once again the extremists have employed virtually every technique possible, from fear tactics to boycotts, in an effort to delay, or in reality prevent implementation of the Belfast Agreement. The Northern Ireland power-sharing Assembly was seated in early 2000, but was suspended when the Unionists withdrew their support and participants (basically the same strategy employed throughout the history of partitioning since the Anglo-Irish treaty of 1921). As of 2006, this has happened on at least four separate occasions with regard to the Belfast Agreement, and it is quite evident now that the unionists view an inevitable re-unification and will do all things necessary to prevent even a first step towards power sharing. Most recently many talks have begun between the other interested factions, basically bypassing the Unionists and their delaying tactics.

Despite all the subversive efforts, the Peace Process moves forward and it is inevitable that the truthful desires of the people will eventually prevail in Northern Ireland, as it should in all other parts of the world. What will it take for this to be accomplished? It will take, as is presently happening, the brave men and women in Northern Ireland, Britain, and the Republic of Ireland to step forward, put the past behind them, and make a concerted effort to work for a better future world; and, identify and hold responsible the groups of "thugs" who continue to undermine the Peace Process.

American Senator George Mitchell, working closely with peace orientated politicians on both sides, spent years laboring on the Northern Ireland peace negotiations and actually drafted the very first rendering of the Belfast Agreement (also known as the Good Friday Agreement). He delivered a most comprehensive speech in September 2001 at St. Bartholomew's Center for Religious Inquiry in New York, outlining many important points regarding the situation in Northern Ireland. He first pointed out that the cooperative efforts between the concerned governments (primarily Britain and the Republic of Ireland), as well as among the local politicians, have been outstanding in spite of what is often reported. He also noted that they are under extreme pressures from certain elements wanting to undermine the peace process, and that it will most likely take an entirely new generation of leaders working towards peace from the onset to dramatically move forward and attempt to put past animosities behind; and, this leadership is most important and essential to instilling the wide spread social belief in peace.

Senator Mitchell further stated that he believed peace is now imminent in Northern Ireland, as the vast majority on both sides does not wish to return to conflict, even though they may strongly want the negotiations to end on favorable terms for their position. Hope further lies in the fact that the overwhelming majority of the inhabitants of this island are intelligent, well informed, honest, friendly, hospitable, and loving people with one of the world's highest literacy rates. Many are beginning to work together, disregarding their differences, in an effort to promote good, as is evidenced by the new political party, the Northern Ireland Women's Coalition Party, which is comprised of mothers on both sides attempting to secure a better world for their children. (Note: Up until quite recently approximately 98% of the children of Northern Ireland have attended religiously segregated schools, and most had never even met those from the other side, at least until after their school years were completed. In an atmosphere such as this it is apparent that stereotypes and mistrust would abound. Those not wanting the peace process to be successful exploit these fears and stereotypes.)

Senator Mitchell concluded by outlining the three relatively minor issues yet to be resolved, the decommissioning of weapons by all paramilitary groups, the demilitarization of Northern Ireland, and the restructuring of the Northern Ireland Police Force; and, by stating that "all conflicts can be resolved by men as they were begun by men, and that we must never submit to men of violence". All of these issues are currently being addressed and moving progressively forward.

Addressing many of the human emotional scars may certainly not be quite as easy. The pains of this long historical conflict are extensive and quite personal to nearly all in Northern Ireland, and nearly everyone must overcome deeply imbedded feelings of mistrust, and even hatred, to reach a place of acceptance and peace. Perhaps we must contemplate and understand by asking such philosophical questions as, what is the true manner of much of mankind? Could it be that throughout history many of the more intelligent, peaceful, kind, loving, and gentle people have often been dominated, even eliminated, by the aggressive and violent elements? Mankind's history is certainly quite violent throughout. What is the true nature of many of the humans having now evolved? Do we now have a more violent and aggressive gene pool base, and how do we now show those with violent tendencies the value of peaceful coexistence in a world becoming smaller and smaller? What is the elemental and/or specifically defined nature of perhaps much deeper personal and social problems we must address and resolve? Human conflict is always complex, but in a land known for saints and scholars a solution could possibly produce an admirable and profound revelation applicable to the positive enhancement of all mankind worldwide.

The world is moving forward at an astounding pace with unlimited opportunities for positive advancement presenting possibilities daily. Ireland has become a world leader in the areas of computer software and information technology. The future prospects and benefits in these areas can hardly yet be imagined. It is vitally important to grasp these positive possibilities of the future and put past evils and animosities at rest behind. And this is in fact being done in Ireland at an impressive rate.

Early in 2001, Pope John Paul II elevated the Irish Archbishop, Desmond Connell, to the College of Cardinals, and one of his very first actions was to gather all the various religious elements of Ireland together in conference at Christ Church Cathedral in Dublin, in an effort to promote unity in Ireland. It was attended by representatives of the Greek Orthodox Church, the Methodist Church, the Lutheran Church, the Catholic Church, the Church of Ireland, and others, with Cardinal Connell stating that one of his main priorities was to bring all these factions together in an effort to promote discourse and understanding. This could be one very important step.

It also leads to another discussion centered on the importance, or relevancy, of our own spiritual beliefs as they relate to our individual perceptions, and our approach to those around us. Catholics and Protestants (as well as Muslims, Jews, Hindus and Buddhists) are taught to Love, Be Compassionate, Merciful, Honest, and Forgiving of those who persecute and wrong you. These are important concepts that generally allow one the spiritual power to grow and have a positive influence on others. It takes a special kind of man or woman to step forward; but, when they do, they bring honor to all about them. This "Honor", based on Truth, was seen by our ancient Irish ancestors as being the essence of all life, and should in fact be our guiding hope and foundation for a most positive future existence.

Ulick O'Connor, perhaps Ireland's greatest living literary figure, discusses the historical perspectives of the Irish Literary Renaissance in the Waterfront Pub, Rosses Point.

Shea Given, perhaps the world's best goalkeeper.

Appendix A

Important Dates in Irish History:

c. 8000 B.C.E.	- Earliest Inhabitants
c. 3700 B.C.E.	- First Neolithic Peoples Arrived
c. 2000 B.C.E.	- Gold Discovered in Wicklow Mountains Bronze Age peoples flourish—build many stone tombs
c. 1100 B.C.E.	- First Celtic Tribes Arrived—The Milesians and Gaels
100 C.E.	- Ptolemy writes about Ireland
432	- St. Patrick returned to Ireland as Bishop
c. 485	- St. Brendan "The Navigator" Born
521	- Colmcille (St. Columba) Born
550–650	- Irish Monasticism flourishes
563	- Iona is founded by St. Columba
590	- Columbanus carries mission to the continent
597	- Death of Colmcille
700–800	- Christian-Gaelic "Golden Age" (Books of Kells, Armagh, and Durrow)
794	- Norse (Vikings) First Come to Ireland
837	- Norse Found Dublin
847	- Danes Invade Ireland
914	- Danes Burn Clonmacnoise
941	- Brian Boru Born
1004	- Brian Boru Became High King of Ireland
1014	- Battle of Clontarf—Irish Victory over Norsemen Brian Boru is killed
1101	- King O'Brien grants Rock of Cashel to the church
1142	- First Cistercian Monastery at Mellifont
1170	- Arrival of Earl of Pembroke (Strongbow)

1171	- King Henry II, Norman King of England Invaded Ireland
1254	- Lordship of Ireland granted to Edward I while he was still a Prince
1307	- Edward I died, Edward II continued to drain Irish resources
1315	- Scots led by Robert and Edward Bruce land at Larne to ally with Ulster Irish
1316	- Battle of Athenry—five Irish kings and numerous chieftains slain
1318	- Battle of Dysert O'Dea (Lord Richard de Clare killed)
1319	- Edward Bruce claims title "King of Ireland"—killed at Faughart, Co. Louth
1327	- Edward II died—half of Irish colonized lands owned by absentee landlords
1366	- Kilkenny Statutes written
1485	- Henry VII ascends to throne of England
1494	- Sir Edward Poynings sent to Ireland to establish King's Parliament
1509	- Accession of Henry VIII to throne of England
1513	- Gerait Og "Ninth Earl of Kildare" Appt. Lord Deputy by Henry VIII
1558	- Death of Queen Mary—Accession of Elizabeth I
1592	- Queen Elizabeth I founded Trinity College
1601	- Battle of Kinsale—4000 troops sent by King Philip III of Spain
1603	- Queen Elizabeth I died. James VI of Scotland became James I of England
1607	- "Flight of the Earls" "Ulster Plantation" established by King James I
1633	- Thomas Wentworth Becomes Governor of Ireland
1641	- The Rising of 1641. "Popish Massacre".
1642	- English Civil War
1649	- English Parliamentary Roundheads Victorious. Oliver Cromwell sent to Ireland. Charles I beheaded.
1652–1654	- Ireland and Scotland Defeated. "Great Britain" formed
1658	- Cromwell Died.
1685	- Catholic James II Became King of England

1688	- "Glorious Revolution". James II fled to France, then Ireland
1689	- William III and Mary II enthroned as joint monarchs in England
1690	- Battle of the Boyne River. James II vs. William of Orange.
1691	- Treaty of Limerick
1695	- First "Penal Laws" enacted
1713	- Jonathan Swift becomes Dean of St. Patrick's Cathedral
1791	- Society of United Irishmen formed by Theobald Wolfe Tone
1795	- "Orange Order" and "The Defenders" organized
1798	- Rising of 1798 (Wexford Rising) Wolfe Tone arrested and sentenced to death
1800	- Act of Union passed (enacted 1 January, 1801)
1823	- Daniel O'Connell forms Catholic Association
1829	- Catholic Emancipation—Catholics could take seats in Parliament
1837	- Accession of Queen Victoria to English throne
1840	- Daniel O'Connell organizes Repeal Association
1842	- Young Irelanders publish first issue of "The Nation"
1845	- Blight of potato crop is beginning of Great Famine
1846	- Corn Laws Repealed
1847–1849	- Worst years of famine "Great Hunger"—over one million die
1856	- "Phoenix Society" founded at Skibbereen (precursor of Fenian movement)
1858	- James Stephens founds Irish Republican Brotherhood Fenian Brotherhood founded in America
1863	- "The Irish People" newspaper founded
1865	- William Butler Yeats born
1867	- Disestablishment of Church of Ireland
1873	- Home Rule League formed
1875	- Charles Stewart Parnell elected MP from County Meath
1880	- Parnell elected Chairman of Irish Parliamentary Party

1884	- Gaelic Athletic Association founded
1886	- First Home Rule Bill introduced by Gladstone
1890	- National Museum of Ireland founded
1891	- Second Home Rule Bill introduced Formation of The Gaelic League (Conradh na Gaelige)
1892	- National Literary Society formed by W.B. Yeats, Lady Augusta Gregory, and Douglas Hyde
1896	- James Connolly forms Irish Republican Socialist Party
1899	- "United Irishman" newspaper founded by Arthur Griffith
1900	- Cumann na nGaedhael Party formed by Arthur Griffith
1903	- Abbey Theatre founded by W.B. Yeats and Lady Gregory
1905	- Sinn Fein founded
1907	- Dockers' strike and riots in Belfast. Riots in Dublin after J. M. Synge's *The Playboy of the Western World* opens.
1909	- Land Purchase Act introduced
1912	- Third Home Rule Bill introduced and passed by House of Commons
1913	- Ulster Volunteer Force established Irish Citizen Army and Irish National Volunteers formed
1914	- Home Rule Act passed, but suspended due to WW I
1916	- Easter Rising in Dublin followed by executions
1917	- Sinn Fein party defeats Parliamentary party in Irish elections
1919	- Dail Eireann meets in Dublin
1919–1921	- Irish War of Independence
1920	- First Black and Tans arrive—"Bloody Sunday"
1921	- Anglo-Irish Treaty providing for Irish Free State and Northern Ireland
1922	- Treaty narrowly approved by Dail, provisional government formed by Collins.
1922–1923	- Irish Civil War
1923	- William Butler Yeats wins Nobel Prize for Literature
1925	- George Bernard Shaw wins Nobel Prize for Literature

1926	- Eamon de Valera leaves Sinn Fein and forms Fianna Fail
1931	- Autonomy of Irish Free State extended by Statute of Westminster
1933	- Fine Gael party formed
1937	- Constitution of Eire—Articles 2 and 3 lay claim also to the Six Counties
1939	- WW II Begins, Eire declares neutrality Death of William Butler Yeats
1941	- German air raids in Derry and Belfast. Death of James Joyce.
1942	- *The Great Hunger* by Patrick Kavanagh
1945	- WW II ends
1949	- Republic of Eire (Ireland) founded
1949	- Ireland Act. UK assures partition would be continued.
1952	- *Waiting For Godot* by Samuel Beckett
1966	- Anglo-Irish Free Trade Agreement Ulster Volunteer Force outlawed
1968	- Civil Rights marches begin in Belfast and Derry
1969	- Samuel Beckett wins Nobel Prize for Literature
1970	- Social Democratic and Labor Party founded. I.R.A. splits into "Provisional I.R.A." and "Official I.R.A."
1971	- Britain agrees to Northern Ireland Internment-1576 people interned. Democratic Unionist Party founded by Ian Paisley.
1972	- "Bloody Sunday" in Derry. Direct Rule imposed by Britain.
1973	- Republic of Ireland and U.K. join European Economic Community
1975	- Northern Ireland Convention convened. Internment suspended
1976	- British Ambassador killed in Dublin
1979	- Earl Mountbatten killed in County Sligo
1980	- *Translations* by Brian Friel performed in Derry
1981	- Death of Bobby Sands and nine other hunger strikers at Long Kesh prison.
1985	- Anglo-Irish Agreement at Hillsborough promotes Protestant backlash
1990	- IRA suspected bombing of London Stock Exchange
1991	- IRA suspected mortar bombing of 10 Downing Street

1994	- First IRA ceasefire
1995	- Seamus Heaney wins Nobel Prize for Literature
1998	- Belfast Agreement (Good Friday Agreement) written
1999	- People in both Republic of Ireland and Northern Ireland approve Belfast Agreement in referendums
2000	- Power-sharing Northern Ireland Assembly established
2000–2006	- Unionists of Northern Ireland employ a variety of tactics to block implementation of Northern Ireland Assembly, and refuse to allow their delegates to be seated. IRA continues ceasefire and decommissioning.

Appendix B

Poblacht na hÉireann

The Provisional Government of the Irish Republic

To the People of Ireland:

Irishmen and Irishwomen! In the name of God and of the dead generations from which she receives the old tradition of nationhood, Ireland, through us, summons her children to her flag, and strikes for her freedom...

We declare the right of the people of Ireland to the ownership of Ireland, and to the unfettered control of Irish destinies, to be sovereign and indefeasible.... In every generation the Irish people have asserted their right to National freedom and sovereignty; six times during the past three hundred years they have asserted it in arms. Standing on that fundamental right and again asserting it in arms in the face of the world, we hereby proclaim the Irish Republic as a Sovereign Independent State, and we pledge our lives and the lives of our comrades to the cause of its freedom, of its welfare, and of its exaltation among the nations....

The Republic guarantees civil and religious liberty, equal rights and equal opportunities to all its citizens, and declares its resolve to pursue the happiness and prosperity of the whole nation and all its parts, cherishing all the children of the nation equally, and oblivious to the differences carefully fostered by an alien government, which have divided a minority from the majority in the past....

We place the cause of the Irish Republic under the protection of the Most High God, whose blessings we invoke upon our arms.... In this supreme hour the Irish nation must, by its valour and discipline, and by the readiness of its children, to sacrifice themselves for the common good, prove itself worthy of the august destiny to which it is called.

Signed on behalf of the Provisional Government,

Thomas J. Clarke,

Sean MacDiarmada,   Thomas MacDonagh,

P. H. Pearse,   Eamonn Ceannt,

James Connolly,   Joseph Plunkett.

APPENDIX C
The Irish Tricolour Flag

The tricolour flag is a rectangle with its width being twice its height. The three colours are of equal size with green being next to the staff. The tricolour flag was first introduced by Thomas Francis Meagher in 1848 as an emblem of the Young Irelanders movement. It was patterned after the French tricolour, representative of that nation's revolution, and was often flown at the Young Irelanders' secret meetings right along side the French tricolour. The green represents the old Irish and Gaelic people, while the orange represents the newer protestant transplanted stock following the Ulster Plantation of James I., and the Williamite Wars. The white in the middle is supposed to represent a lasting truce and peace between the two. When Meagher introduced the flag he stated, "The white in the center signifies a lasting truce between the 'Orange' and the 'Green' and I trust that beneath its folds the hands of the Irish Protestant and the Irish Catholic may be clasped in heroic brotherhood".

During the Rising of 1916 it was flown above the General Post Office and other buildings; and, from that time on it has been regarded as the National flag of the Republic of Ireland. This was formalized as such by the Constitution of 1937.

Appendix D

The Irish Harp: a historical discussion

Ireland is the only country in the world that has a musical instrument as its national emblem. When the harp was incorporated into the state seal of the Irish Free State in 1922, its designer, Mr. George Sigerson wrote, "It is now within the power of an Irish independent government to replace this emblem of humanizing harmony in its high place of honour, unique and not undistinguished amongst the lions, the leopards, and the single and double-headed eagles of the rest of the world."

The Irish harp, in its distinctive shape, has been the major symbol and characteristic musical instrument of Ireland since at least the twelfth century. The precise early history of the harp has become obscure, although it most probably evolved from the prehistoric lyre, which dates back to ancient Sumeria. The triangular harp, also known as the frame harp, is a distinctly European invention, most probably originating among the Celtic peoples. From the earliest times this harp has developed a distinctive form, as well as a distinctive social role in Ireland. It has played a prominent role in Irish life since the earliest historical accounts, and these accounts claim roots much further back into Irish mythology and folklore.

Irish mythology is full of stories regarding harps and harpers. Dagda, the main god of Irish and Gaelic mythology and head of the people known as the Tuatha de Danann, was known to have been able to play three types of magical music on the harp. He first played to ease the pain of others, especially his wife Boann (namesake of the Boyne River) who suffered greatly during childbirth. He could also play a magical music that could put his enemies to sleep on the battlefield (he used this talent on several different occasions against his main enemies, the Fomhoraigh people). He also played a magical music that facilitated the spiritual travel of souls and shape-shifters from this world to the otherworld, and back.

The harper Craiftine appears in a number of ancient stories. The most famous of which deals with the mythological king of Leinster, Labhraidh Loingseach and dates back to the early tenth century. Apparently, the king had the ears of a horse and every time he got his hair cut, the barber had to be put to death to keep from letting this secret out. Supposedly at one point the king could no longer keep the secret himself and confided in a certain willow tree. Craiftine came along and cut this very willow tree to make a new harp; and, everytime he played this new harp, it would sing, "King Labhraidh has horse ears".

Poets and musicians, especially harpers, held a place of great honour in early Irish society, both pagan and early Christian. In pre-Christian Ireland, music was practiced as being divine, facilitating travel between this world and the spirit world, or otherworld. According to the Feineachas (or Brehon Laws) the harpers held the highest social standing among all musicians, and this remained so until well into the seventeenth century. In the Book of the Four Masters, "Annala Riochta Eireann", written in 1636, the authors offer detailed accounts regarding the deaths of generations of individual harpers, listed chronologically and by name.

Following the Battle of Kinsale (1601), and the coming of Cromwell (1649), the native Irish order and traditional society began to change dramatically. By the end of the seventeenth century, the remaining traditional Irish harpers became little more than itinerant musicians who traveled from one patron's home to another. By the beginning of the nineteenth century even this lifestyle was unable to survive, and the making and playing of traditional Irish harps, as it had been known for over two thousand years, eventually all but died out.

The harp is once again today becoming more popular, but the modern harp, sometimes called the "neo-Irish harp", is not quite the same instrument as the ancient harp, neither in construction nor method of playing.

The Harp as a Symbol of Ireland

The harp is represented often in the oldest illuminated manuscripts and on the great High Crosses, dating back to at least the eighth century. The harp pictured at that time was never shown standing alone, it was always shown being played, and was believed to represent the Hebrew King David of prehistoric Torah and Biblical fame.

The first time the harp appeared as a symbolic graphic representation of the country of Ireland came in the late thirteenth century. It appeared in a French manuscript now known as The Wijnbergen Armorial (named for its present owners). An Armorial, or what was also called a Roll of Arms, was a manuscript illustrating the coats of arms and/or family crests of all the feudal lords and knights of a particular area or region. These were also developed to illustrate all the lords and knights that participated in a given war, or were even present at a particular battle. The second part of this particular manuscript includes the coat of arms for all the various kings, and near the end there is a coat of arms attributed to *le.Roi dirlande (The King of Ireland)*. It consists of a yellow harp with eight white strings on a blue shield. This manuscript was apparently compiled by a French Herald serving in the court of King Philipe III le Hardi, and dates from between 1270 and 1285. The dating of this manuscript places the Irish Harp as being among the ten oldest national symbols of today's world. The style of the harp is the same as those that had long been represented in ancient Ireland.

Historians are not certain where this particular coat of arms originated, as there was no "King of Ireland" at that particular time; and, in fact there was no state or nation of Ireland displaying such a symbol. There is a theory that the English monarchy may have devised the coat of arms to identify their dominions or territories; but, there is no historical evidence to substantiate this belief. It is well known however that the harp was widely accepted at that time as being the symbol for Ireland.

Many tenth, eleventh and twelfth century writers associated the harp with Ireland, including John of Salisbury, the English priest and philosopher who eventually became the Bishop of Chartres. He wrote from approximately 1120 to 1180, and stated there would not have been any music on the crusades at all if it were not for the Irish harp. Interestingly enough, this is also virtually the only historical evidence indicating the Irish took any part whatsoever in the crusades. Giraldus Cambrensis, the Norman/Welsh priest and nephew of Maurice Fitzgerald who wrote in the twelfth century, described the harp and its music in great detail in his work *Topographia Hibernica.*

It was not until the late fifteenth century that the harp emblem was definitively used by England to represent its territorial claims to Ireland. Earlier, from approximately 1386, when Robert de Vere was named Duke of Ireland by King Richard II of England, Ireland was represented by three small yellow crowns on a blue shield with a white border. This emblem was used to represent Ireland until around 1487. One historian of the nineteenth century, Bernard Burke, claims the Norman/English used this coat of arms to represent Ireland ever since the initial invasion of Henry II in 1172.

At the College of Arms in London there is a painting and manuscript from 1531-1532, signifying the coat of arms of Ireland as being the gold harp on a blue shield. The endeavor that led to widespread recognition of the harp as symbolizing Ireland however, came at the hands of the notorious Henry VIII. He used the Irish harp as a motif on the Anglo-Irish silver coins known as the groat (four pence) and the half-groat (two pence). He initiated this coinage in 1534/1535. This was also the first time that the harp appeared under a crown, and the crowned harp remained on Anglo-Irish coinage up until 1826. After that year a separate British coinage for Ireland no longer existed.

The harp was even more firmly established as the symbol for Ireland in 1541 when Henry VIII converted Ireland from a "lordship" to the "Kingdom of Ireland" and devised a new coat of arms; and, from then on the harp was widely recognized as representing Ireland. It was a gold harp on a blue shield that graced John Goghe's map of Ireland in 1567. This same harp symbol was also displayed by Queen Elizabeth I during her pilgrimage to the city of Dublin in 1583, and then again in 1588, on the charts produced by Augustine Ryther showing the routes of the Spanish Armada before their defeat. A blue flag with a yellow harp was carried at the funeral of Queen Elizabeth I in 1603. King James I then incorporated the yellow harp on a blue field into the British Royal Arms and Standard in 1603, and it has remained the same ever since. It was not until 1945 however that the harp was adopted by the Irish Free State as the official coat of arms.

The harp on the green flag background first appeared in 1642, flown by Eoghan Rua O'Neill, who had left Ireland in 1607 during the "Flight of the Earls". He returned in 1642 to lead the Ulster Irishmen in the insurrection that had broken out in 1641. His frigate flew the yellow harp on a green flag as an act of defiance against England. Since 1644, the yellow harp on a green field has been the symbol for the province of Leinster, and was in effect the flag flown representing the country of Ireland until the Tricolour was adopted during the Eater Rising in 1916. (Cromwell's armies carried flags with the harp on a blue field, and also on a red field.)

Green had long been associated with Ireland due to its lush vegetation, particularly in literature and folklore. The literary usage culminated in 1795 when William Drennan termed Ireland the "Emerald Isle" in his poem "Erin". In 1670 the colour green became for the first time associated with St. Patrick and his story of the shamrock, and by 1730 green crosses were being worn on St. Patrick's Day.

The harp on a green background was solidified as a national symbol for Ireland when it was adopted by the Society of United Irishmen on their flags and seal in 1791, and then flown in the rising of 1798. Theobald Wolfe Tone wrote in his diary on 23 June 1796, that he had discussed this Irish flag with the French and other European governments and it was from then on to be recognized as the national flag. From this time forward green was even further associated with nationalist Ireland through the writing of patriotic songs, such as "The Wearing of the Green" and "Seanbhean Bhocht".

In 1803 Robert Emmet attempted to continue the revolution that had been begun by the United Irishmen. On his flag he added a banner that read "Erin go bragh" (Ireland forever). The green flag, in one form or another, has been used by virtually every Irish social and political movement since, ie The Repeal Association, Young Ireland, the Irish Republican Brotherhood, The Fenians, the Home Rule movements, the Land League, the Irish Volunteers, The Irish Citizen Army, etc., etc.

By 1917, the Tricolour flag had replaced the harp flag. The Tricolour was first seen, in one form or another, from around 1830. In 1848, John Mitchel proposed that it be adopted as the national flag in an article in the *United Irishman* newspaper. From that time on it was used to a limited extent, and was generally considered to be more revolutionary and more republican than the green harp flag. In 1916, the Tricolour seemed to capture the mood of the times. Unlike the harp flag, it had arisen out of a totally nationalistic movement, and had a rather explicit reference to the French revolution. The Tricolour became the definitive revolutionary symbol as it flew above the General Post Office on Dublin's Sackville Street (now O'Connell Street) during the Easter Rising, and was used almost exclusively from that time onward. It was adopted as the official flag of the Irish

Free State in 1922, and the Constitution of 1937 declared it as the national flag of Ireland. Some say the green-harp flag may be a consideration for a reintegrated/united thirty-two county Ireland. The harp emblem is still used today on state seals, the presidential seal, money, and the official coat of arms of the Republic of Ireland adopted in 1945. Many Irish institutions, corporations, and businesses including the Bank of Ireland, the National Gallery of Ireland, and others have incorporated the harp into their seals or logos as well.

APPENDIX E

Republic of Ireland Population by Provinces and Counties:

	1926	1991	2002
Republic of Ireland	(2,971,992)	(3,525,719)	(3,917,336)
Province of Leinster	(1,149,092)	(1,860,949)	(2,105,449)
County		Population	
	(1926)	(1991)	(2002)
Carlow	34,476	40,946	45,845
Dublin	505,654	1,024,429	1,122,600
Kildare	58,028	122,516	163,995
Kilkenny	70,990	73,613	80,421
Laoighis	51,540	52,325	58,732
Longford	39,847	30,293	31,127
Louth	62,739	90,707	101,802
Meath	62,969	105,540	133,936
Offaly	52,592	58,448	63,702
Westmeath	56,818	61,882	72,027
Wexford	95,848	102,045	116,543
Wicklow	57,591	97,293	114,719

Province of Munster (969,902) (1,009,533) (1,101,266)

	(1926)	(1991)	(2002)
Clare	95,064	90,826	103,333
Cork	365,747	409,814	448,181
Kerry	149,171	121,719	132,424
Limerick	140,343	161,856	175,529

Tipperary N.	59,645	57,854	61,068
Tipperary S.	81,370	74,918	79,213
Waterford	78,582	91,608	101,518

Province of Connacht (552,907) (423,031) (464,050)

Galway	169,366	180,304	208,826
Leitrim	55,907	25,297	25,815
Mayo	172,690	110,696	117,428
Roscommon	83,556	51,876	53,803
Sligo	71,388	54,736	58,178

Province of Ulster (part of) (300,091) (232,206) (246,571)

Cavan	82,452	52,756	56,594
Donegal	152,506	127,994	137,383
Monaghan	65,131	51,262	52,772

*Taken from 2002 Census, Preliminary Report, Table 1

APPENDIX F

Political Makeup of the 29th Dail

The 29th Dail has 166 deputies returned by 42 constituencies. The following is the position of political parties as returned in the General Election (17 May 2002):

Fianna Fail	81
Fine Gael	31
Labour	21
Progressive Democrats	8
Green Party	6
Sinn Fein	5
Socialist Party	1
Others	13

* Taken from *Nealon's Guide to the 29th Dail & Seanad, Geraldine Kennedy (ed.).*

References/Further Reading

Adams, Gerry Free Ireland: Towards a Lasting Peace. Roberts Rinehart Publishers, Niwot, Colorado. 1994.

Adams, Gerry Hope and History: Making Peace in Ireland. Brandon Mount Eagle Publications, Dingle, County Kerry, Ireland

Asplin, P. W. A. Medieval Ireland c.1170-1495: A Bibliography of Secondary Works. Royal Irish Academy, Dublin. 1971.

Beiler, Ludwig Ireland, Harbinger of the Middle Ages. Oxford. 1963.

Byrne, Francis John Irish Kings and High-Kings. London. 1973

Cahill, Thomas How the Irish Saved Civilization: The Untold Story of Ireland's Heroic Role from the Fall of Rome To the Rise of Medieval Europe. Doubleday, New York. 1995.

Davies, Norman The Isles: A History. Oxford University Press, Oxford. 1999.

de Paor, Liam St. Patrick's World. Dublin. 1993.

de Paor, Liam Ireland and Early Europe. Dublin. 1997.

Department of Foreign Affairs Facts About Ireland. Government of Ireland, Dublin. 1995.

Dillon, Myles (ed.) Early Irish Society (Thomas Davis Lectures). Dublin. 1954.

Duffy, Kevin Who Were the Celts? Barnes and Noble Books, New York. 1996.

Duncan, Anthony The Elements of Celtic Christianity. Element Books Limited, Shaftesbury, Dorset. 1992.

Dunne, John J. Shrines Of Ireland. Veritas Publications, Dublin. 1989.

Foster, Robert Fitzroy (ed.) The Oxford Illustrated History of Ireland. Oxford University Press, Oxford. 1989.

Fry, Plantagenet and Fiona Somerset The History of Scotland. Routledge and Kegan, London. 1982.

Gallagher, Meadbh In, *An Phoblacht/Republican News,* 7 September 1995.

Gregory, Lady Augustus Cuchulain and Muirthemne. John Murray Publishers, London. 1902.

Gregory, Lady Augustus Gods and Fighting Men. John Murray Publishers, London. 1904.

Henry, Francoise Irish Art In the Early Christian Period (to 800 A.D.) London. 1965.

Hughes, Kathleen The Church In Early Irish Society. London. 1966.

Hughes, Kathleen and Ann Hamlin The Modern Traveller to the Early Irish Church. London. 1977.

Hyde, Douglas A Literary History of Ireland. London. 1899.

Kelly, Fergus A Guide to Early Irish Law. Dublin. 1988.

Kelly, Fergus Early Irish Farming: A Study Based Mainly on the Law-texts of the 7th and 8th Centuries A.D. Dublin. 1997.

Kennedy, Geraldine (ed.) Nealon's Guide to the 29th Dail & Seanad. Gill and Macmillan Ltd., Dublin 12. 2002.

Kenny, Michael The Fenians. The National Museum of Ireland, Dublin. 1994.

Litton, Helen The Irish Civil War: An Illustrated History. Wolfhound Press Ltd. Dublin 1. 1995

Lucas, A. T. Cattle In Ancient Ireland. Kilkenny. 1989.

Mac Annaidh, Seamas Irish History. Parragon Books, Bath, UK. 2001.

Mac Cana, Proinseas Celtic Mythology. London. 1970.

Mac Niocaill, Gearoid Ireland Before the Vikings (Gill History of Ireland I). Dublin. 1972.

Maclean, Magnus The Literature of the Celts. Blackie and Son Ltd., London. 1902.

MacManus, Seumas The Story of the Irish Race. Random House, New York. 1990.

McCormack, W. J. Ascendancy and Tradition in Anglo-Irish Literary History from 1789 to 1939. Oxford University Press, Oxford. 1985.

Metress, Seamus P. The Hunger Strike and the Final Struggle. Connolly Books, Detroit. 1983.

Metress, Seamus P. Outlines in Irish History: Eight Hundred Years of Struggle, Connolly Books, Detroit. 1995.

Metress, Seamus P. and Molly Schiever (eds.) The Irish In Toledo: History and Memory. University of Toledo Urban Affairs Center Press. 2005.

Monk, Michael A. and John Sheehan (ed.) Early Medieval Munster Archaeology, History and Society. Cork University Press, Cork. 1998.

Mullan, Don The Dublin and Monaghan Bombings. Wolfhound Press Ltd., Dublin 1. 2000.

Murphy, Gerard The Ossianic Lore and Romantic Tales of Medieval Ireland. Cultural Relations Committee, Dublin. 1955.

O'Brien, Maire and Conor Cruise A Concise History of Ireland. Beekman House, New York. 1972.

O Corrain, Donnchadh Ireland Before the Normans (Gill History of Ireland II). Dublin. 1972.

O Croinin, Daibhi Early Medieval Ireland, 400-1200. London. 1995.

O Danachair, Caoimhin The Nine Irons, Festchrift fur Robert Wildhaber. Basel. 1973, pp. 471-476.

O'Ferrall, Fergus Catholic Emancipation: Daniel O'Connell and the Birth of Irish Democracy. Dublin. 1985.

Piehler, H. A. Ireland For Everyman. W. W. Norton and Company, New York. 1961.

Pollard, H. B. C. The Secret Societies of Ireland: Their Rise and Progress. The Irish Historical Press, Kilkenny. 1998.

Reeves-Smyth, Terence and Fred Hammond Landscape Archaeology In Ireland. British Archaeology Reports, Oxford. 1983.

Rodgers, Michael and Marcus Losack Glendalough: A Celtic Pilgrimage. The Columba Press, Dublin. 1998.

Ryan, Meda The Day Michael Collins Was Shot. Poolbeg Press Ltd., Dublin. 1989.

Ryan, Michael Ireland and Insular Art: A.D. 500-1200. Royal Irish Academy, Dublin. 1985.

Rynne, Etienne The Art of Early Irish Illumination. The Capuchin Annual, Vol. 36. 1969.

Rynne, Etienne The Revival of Irish Art in the Late 19th and Early 20th Century. In: Themes In Irish Culture, Topic 24, Washington and Jefferson College, Washington, Pa. 1972.

Rynne, Etienne The Swastika at Ennis—Symbol of the Resurrection. North Munster Antiquarian Journal, 32. 1990, pp. 3-18.

Rynne, Etienne Dun Aengus and some similar Celtic Ceremonial Centres, In: Bernelle, Agnes (ed.) Decantations, A Tribute to Maurice Craig. Dublin. 1992, pp. 196-207.

Rynne, Etienne A Pagan Celtic Background for Sheela-na-Gigs? In: Archaeologia Cambrensis. 2000.

Saint Benedict A Rule for Beginners. Order of Saint Benedict, Collegeville, Minn. 1981.

Sands, Bobby One Day in My Life. Mercier Press, Dublin 2. 1983.

Sawyer, Peter Kings and Vikings: Scandanavia and Europe AD 700-1100. London. 1982.

Scherman, Katharine The Flowering of Ireland: Saints, Scholars, And Kings. Barnes and Noble Books, New York. 1996.

Simms, J. G. Jacobite Ireland 1685-1691. London. 1969.

Thomas, Charles And Shall These Mute Stones Speak? Post-Roman Inscriptions In Western Wales. Cardiff. 1994.

Thomson, David and Moyra McGusty (eds.) The Irish Journals of Elizabeth Smith 1840-1850. Oxford University Press, Oxford. 1980.

Wall, Maureen The Penal Laws. Irish Royal Historical Society, Dublin. 1961.

Wallace, Martin A Short History of Ireland. Barnes and Noble Books, New York. 1996.

Whitelock, Dorothy and Rosamond McKitterick and David Dumville (eds.) Ireland In Early Medieval Europe. Cambridge University Press, Cambridge. 1982.

Woodham-Smith, Cecil The Great Hunger: Ireland 1845-1949. Harper and Roe, Publishers, New York and Evanston. 1962.

Yeats, William Butler (ed.) Fairy and Folk Tales of Ireland. Colin Smythe Gerrards Cross, Buckinghamshire. 1973.

978-0-595-38985-8
0-595-38985-6